D1328412

DETROIT INDUSTRIAL
MISSION
A PERSONAL NARRATIVE

. . . for we cannot but speak of what we have seen and heard.
—Acts 4:20

DETROIT INDUSTRIAL MISSION

A PERSONAL NARRATIVE

SCOTT I. PARADISE

HARPER & ROW, PUBLISHERS

NEW YORK, EVANSTON, AND LONDON

1817

To Muffy

CONTENTS

FOREWORD

This is one of the best books written about Christianity in years. It is not a ghettoized, abstract treatise unrelated to life, nor does it succumb to the fashionable and quite momentary avant-garde. The book incarnates struggle, crisis, and tension, as a contemporary Christian priest seeks actually to relate the gospel to modern industrial life.

The result is a quite beautiful book which may, in due time, become a classic. For it is honest amid platitudes, piosity, and propaganda.

Who is Scott Paradise? His directness, clear vocation, personal problems arising out of both secular confrontation and institutional religious opposition, and intense purpose to proclaim the gospel of Jesus: these are reminiscent of the passionate, memorable Jesuit mission into the Chinese realm of another age.

I first met Scott Paradise in Sheffield, England, in 1954. He was an industrial missioner working under then Canon (now Bishop) E. R. Wickham; I was immediately out of a theological seminary in Berkeley, California, and about to jump out of my skin in a desperate search for radical Christian witness in the world. To my surprise, I discovered it in Sheffield.

Wickham, blinking owlishly through the severe frames of his glasses as he introduced me to socially concerned Christians whom I couldn't quite believe, was a startling witness to a contemporary, living Christ; so was my young American peer, Scott, who met me on rainy mornings in front of factories and allowed me to accompany him on his trips to shop floors and his lunch and coffee-break* sessions with workingmen. Too, there were evening meetings where he inveigled me to stand up and speak—with all my mixed feelings of personal inadequacy and bottled-up conviction about the Christ of the worker-priests—in front of English workers.

Scott was marvelously controlled, I thought, as he reacted with extreme interior emotion and exterior cool to people and events surrounding him. I saw him in his digs—a simple room in the working-class section of Sheffield—and in action within his factories and meetings. He deeply affected me: here was a man, with whom I could readily identify in age and feelings, who was translating the most idealistic Christian concepts into everyday activities and witnessing.

His name seemed to be one grasped from pure fiction for a cleric, a divine, a minister, a priest. In any event, Tennessee Williams should have appropriated it long ago for one of his colorful or colorless stage clergymen.

I didn't see Scott again, after my visit to Sheffield, until Detroit in 1960. He had changed, of course. The youthful drive and earnestness were still there, but one could see the maturing effect of suffering and simply living in the Christian tension of acknowledged paradox and comprehended moral ambiguities. Physically, he was much the same, with his urgent smile and tremendous effort to be outgoing in order to stimulate conversation and relationship. Yet his attitudes and words were different. Now they were more sophisticated, better informed, less dogmatic, terribly open-ended to encourage dialogue, and groping for a valid conceptualization of the gospel within this historical period and, indeed, this hour.

We became friends at a much more serious level than before. I was constantly aware of his sensitivity, marked by both joy and pain, beneath the necessary functions of his work. Often we met early in mornings for breakfast chats concerning his crises

---

* These were, in fact, tea-breaks.—Ed.

of faith and practice, and mine; I became closely acquainted in
their home with his wife Muffy and the children, for one of whom
I am a godfather; and, too, Scott and Muffy visited, on several
occasions, my apartment across from Wayne State University,
when, seated on the floor with black nationalists and white liberals,
black bourgeoisie and white radicals, all the stops were pulled
out in hours' long sessions of human confrontation and, sometimes, self-discovery.

I read parts of his Journals then. I found them incredibly
meaningful and also downright hopeless for publication in their
existing disconnected form. Later, I visited Scott and Muffy in
Boston, after they had moved there from Detroit. He had started
to think seriously about revising the Journals, putting them into
book form.

We now have the result of his work. He matter-of-factly tells
his story, that of a modern Christian missioner entering into the
thought forms and technical structures of industry. I suppose it is
his flat, uncompromising honesty which is immediately startling:
one realizes Scott is telling the truth, at considerable cost, for
truth has to be costly. He has given us a solid, unpretentious
document of incalculable value. Church and industrial historians
may well consider it a primary source when they attempt to delve
into the real meanings of our period. Scott, who has studied a
good deal of history, paused long enough in his academic pursuits
to make—and then write—some history of his own. It is exciting
and breaks new ground.

MALCOLM BOYD

Washington, D.C.
December, 1967

PREFACE

The term *industrial mission* was coined by Canon E. R. Wickham, who in 1944 developed a project under the Church of England to relate to the workers and managers of the heavy steel industry in Sheffield, England. The phrase was still new to me and the Sheffield brogue still almost unintelligible when I became the first American on the staff of this mission. Little in my background had led me to anticipate that I would be roaming the long black steel mills and engaging in intense and sometimes hilarious informal discussions with groups of workers gathered in their lean-tos or lunchrooms, next to furnaces or among their machines. It may have been youthful rebelliousness that drove me into such an unexpected role. But my concern about the inability of the Christian faith to bear relevantly on the public issues of modern life was the goad I was aware of at the time.

The face-to-face confrontation with the weakness of the English churches, however, changed my concern to acute anxiety. I was shaken, for instance, to discover that less than one per cent of the Sheffield steelworkers had any ongoing relationship with any church. I was even more dismayed when I experienced the massive indifference of workers and managers alike to any religious claims at all.

Canon Wickham, now Bishop of Middleton in Manchester, established his industrial mission at the invitation of the Bishop of Sheffield in order to bridge this yawning chasm between thriving industry and the feeble churches. Believing that new strategy and a radical reinterpretation of the Christian faith were imperative, he did not try to bring workers into the churches but rather met them on their own industrial ground. Nor did the mission attempt to preach the gospel in traditional terms, but rather listened to the voices in industry and tried through free-for-all discussion to discover arresting and appropriate ways to understand the purposes of God for industrial life.

By the time of my arrival in 1953 the Sheffield Industrial Mission had a full-time staff of four ministers, a hundred regularly meeting discussion groups in mills and offices, and acceptance, trust, and respect at every level of the industry. This and other demonstrations of the possibilities of such a ministry encouraged the Reverend Hugh White of Detroit to establish in 1956 an industrial mission in his home city. I accepted his invitation to join him the next year.

Detroit the reality does not betray Detroit, symbol of twentieth-century mass production. It boasts the birthplace of the moving assembly line and also a level of industrialization unsurpassed anywhere in the world. Though of course the automobile industry giants dominate the city, hundreds of corporations of every possible size are located there, and many scores of medium-sized and large manufacturing plants jostle each other along several industrial corridors within and beyond the city limits. The plants belonging to large companies conform to general policy directives laid down at company headquarters, but very often individual plant managements have a large measure of autonomy in day-to-day operations. They can call, however, for the assistance and counsel of staff specialists from headquarters.

Besides the cars manufactured there, labor relations are a consuming interest in industrial Detroit. The protagonists are the personnel, industrial-relations, or labor-relations managers on the one hand and representatives of the unions on the other. My main contact was with two large industrial unions. In each the top leadership was often referred to as "the International," since both claimed membership in Canada as well as the United States.

Administratively these unions are broken down into regions or
districts which include many locals in neighboring cities. These
often have their own hall, offices, and a full-time elected president,
chief steward, or other officials. Beyond this a thousand flowers
bloom. The largest locals are broken down further into units,
each with its own full-time officials. Some represent all the blue-
collar workers in a single plant; others have workers from several
smaller plants making up their membership. The union officials
on the lowest level who first handle the workers' grievances are
sometimes elected volunteers, but in other plants may be full-time
pro's. These men are usually known as stewards or committeemen.
Very roughly, the organization of these two unions may be said
to run parallel to the organization of the big corporations they
negotiate with. The "International" is comparable to corporate
headquarters, the districts or regions to the company divisions,
and the locals to individual plants. At the bottom, a steward rep-
resents the union in each plant department and deals with the
foremen or supervisors who make up the lowest level of management.

In the course of my experience with the Detroit Industrial
Mission, generally referred to as "D.I.M.," I had regular discussions with groups of managers in a half-dozen different locations
and considerable contact with an equal number of local unions.
Besides this, I was an occasional visitor at both corporate and
International headquarters, and sporadically in many other plants
and union locals. Since the influence of the dominant industry
shapes almost every facet of this city's life, I found myself in
touch with labor relations lawyers, arbitrators, mediators, a group
of advertising men, civil rights organizations, and other groups in
the community at large. This volume, however, deals at length
only with my association with unions, workers, managers, and of
course, the churches.

When I arrived in Detroit, the mission had been in existence
for less than a year. Hugh White was its only full-time employee.

Its tone was distinctly Episcopalian and its activities had centered upon four Episcopal congregations, running the gamut from rich to poor, but all in Detroit's northern or western suburbs. Hugh had already visited many of the men from these "associated parishes" at their places of work and had led them in study and discussion in their parish halls.

With my arrival we strove increasingly to develop relations with groups of men in their work location, studiously ignoring their church affiliation or lack of it. As the months went on this purely industrial orientation of D.I.M. became the major emphasis, although considerable time was always spent with church-based groups. As the work was beginning, Mr. Robert Grindley volunteered much time and energy to the development of the mission. In 1960 the Reverend Robert Batchelder, Congregationalist, joined me as a full-time associate with Hugh White, and later we were further joined by the Reverend Jesse Christman and the Reverend James Campbell. Both of these were Presbyterians, and each came to D.I.M. with a background of four years as a worker on the assembly line. Thus, in the period covered by this volume, the Detroit Mission became increasingly interdenominational in leadership, industrial in orientation, and cooperative in operation.

The book is based on a journal, almost an accidental by-product of my work. I kept it throughout these years, partly perhaps because I did not want to forget what I was learning, and partly, too, because I was often lonely, bewildered, and immersed in a deep sense of conflict. Entries were not made every day, nor always on the day the recorded events happened. But once or twice a week I would write down what I had seen that seemed particularly significant, and my reflections on it. Until very near the end I had no idea of publication, because of the confidential material involved. Yet as the bulk of the accumulating record increased, the realization came that if I deleted repetitions, confidential or uninteresting material, and any passages which might embarrass the continuing work of D.I.M., a useful document might still survive.

I have also carefully changed the names of the people and organizations with which I worked in industry and labor, and disguised some of the events and nomenclature so as to prevent identification. However, a few of those in the churches, the community, and of course in public life still bear their own names.

The journal entries have been edited and grouped in order to make a readable book, with added explanations and identification where necessary, and a rearrangement of the order of some of the entries. These editorial changes leave both the substance of what is described and its chronology very largely unchanged.

I publish this account almost in fear and trembling, partly because I expect it may draw criticism on the grounds that it does not present a balanced or fair picture of how things are in industry or the church. To this I must answer that the story is not a balanced sociological survey but rather a somewhat impressionistic record of my own limited personal experience. Others, I am sure, would and will have other experience. To some the book may seem a little naïve. This I think reflects not so much lack of perception or understanding as the rather private quality of a journal or diary type of record, and also a certain refusal to adopt completely the value assumptions of those in industry who became my friends and acquaintances. From this difference of values at times tension arose between myself and others, and within myself, which I trust was creative.

Finally, it is also possible that the book will be seen as a direct attack upon industry, labor, or the churches. I cannot emphasize too strongly that this is not the case. Indeed, in it I confess our own problems and weaknesses so freely that it might rather be construed as an attack on the whole industrial mission enterprise. But this is obviously not the case, either. Certainly here is something less than a glossy public relations success story.

Yet if it seems to dwell on disappointments, difficulties, and failures as well as the more positive side, this is partly because these are building blocks for the future. If others are to learn from my experience, I must tell it as it was.

My reason for publishing the record is because it reveals something about the condition of us all which is both important and far from adequately recognized. Something akin to what current theological discussion refers to as "the death of God" is concretely documented in this narrative. I hope it may also give a glimmering of a possible awakening of man.

Since hundreds of people in their association with me during these years in Detroit contributed to this book, to acknowledge my debt to them individually would be impossible. For this contribution and especially in many cases for their friendship I can only return my gratitude. I must thank in particular, however, Hugh White and my other colleagues on the D.I.M. staff for their support of me then and now for their willingness to have me publish this book. I owe thanks also to Henry Hager whose interest in my journal led me to begin readying it for publication and to Annabelle Learned whose advice helped me to complete the task.

—Scott I. Paradise

West Newton, Mass.
November, 1967

I
THE WORLD OF LABOR

ONE

☙

THE LEAP

WE FOUND THE union leader sitting behind his desk in his wood-paneled office in union headquarters. He wore an open-necked Hawaiian-type sport shirt on his back, and dark glasses and an inscrutable expression on his face. Three assistants lounged on the overstuffed leather couches along the wall. "Sunshine," he growled at one of them in his Irish brogue, "get us some coffee."

Hugh White and I were there because we had decided that I should try to build an ongoing relationship with a certain big union local, and this official was responsible for the locals of the union in that area. He had known Hugh for some years and had heard about his plans to begin an industrial mission, so he was not surprised when we asked how best to approach the local we had in mind. He said he would help, but warned us to walk circumspectly if we wanted our welcome to last for any length of time.

"That's not only a big local," he said, "but it's politically minded. It has a lot of competing factions. The Masons are banded together as one political group. They're often at odds with the

3

Catholics. Communists have been extremely active there, and the large number of Negroes often function like black chauvinists —that is, they leave aside considerations of policy and personality and vote according to race. When you go into this local, you've got to stay clear of any particular group. Otherwise you'll probably be washed up with all the other groups. Go see Larry Forbes, the recording secretary. He's the most likely to understand what you're up to. I'll call him and see if we can arrange for Sunshine to take you down and see him."

This he did, and so well did Larry and I get along that the first interview lasted many hours and ended (literally) in a fishing expedition. He was interested in my experience in England and questioned me closely about the purposes and goals of industrial mission. Only a few years from retirement, he had spent most of his productive life with one company. Here in the local he had earned both respect and influence, and his vivid stories made its history come alive.

A few days later I phoned him to ask, "Larry, can you arrange an appointment to take me in to meet the president of the local?" He groaned and said, "I don't know. He's a hard man to see. I'll do my best." Twenty minutes later he called back and reported, "Arnie'll see you on Thursday at three-thirty. Come to my office a little before."

The local president, Arnie Leblanc, was a well-known and controversial figure. Some had spoken of his integrity. Others saw him as a Machiavellian opportunist who would stop at nothing to gain his political ends. So when Larry ushered me into his office, I carried a load of curiosity along.

Arnie Leblanc proved to be a young-looking, attractive second-generation French Canadian. He listened attentively while I explained the industrial mission as an attempt to understand the weekday application of such Christian ideas as justice and humanity. These I said were interests the union and the church had in common. I hoped to help make their connection more conscious and apparent, to the benefit of both. At length in a tone of utter sincerity he said, "You know, in my job I'm simply trying to do during the week what you priests and ministers should be preaching on Sunday. What is it you want?"

"I want to get to really know the labor movement," I answered. "What I'd like most is a standing invitation to meetings at the local—" Without hesitation he granted my request, and the interview was over.

The following week I attended the Wednesday afternoon meeting of the local executive board. A few months earlier, Larry told me, a Methodist minister had asked the board to invite him to their meetings. After some debate they refused, for they felt that such closeness to religious moralism incarnate would be more than they could bear. When I arrived, therefore, I rather wondered what welcome I would receive. In the middle of the meeting room fifteen men sat at a big table with Leblanc, Forbes, and the other officers at the head. I joined a few rank-and-file members of the union who sat in folding chairs along the wall. Although my clerical collar caused some to glance at me curiously, Leblanc, who was presiding, did not acknowledge my existence. But Forbes later introduced me and reported that the officers had decided to invite me to attend the meetings at the local in order to discover the truth about the labor movement, and the ways in which the justice and fair play preached about on Sunday can be put to work during the week. To my surprise, and even more my relief, there was no comment, no question, and no vote. Perhaps not yet accepted, at least I was officially admitted.

The winning of this bridgehead occupied only part of my attention. At the same time I was participating in the programs Hugh had begun with four associated church parishes and calling on managers, workers, and union officials from other locations as well. But in the next few weeks I had ample time to attend several meetings of Leblanc's local, two of which had more than a hundred men present. What impressed me was the drama and the conflict.

Through the perpetual haze of tobacco smoke, I grew used to seeing men there with every possible shade of skin, and to hearing the English language spoken with every imaginable accent. One board member known as Mex stood hardly more than five feet four and marched purposefully around the local in an oversized hat. A rank-and-filer with an absolutely naked scalp and an immense stomach often attended meetings dressed in a grubby T-shirt, broken-down shoes, and no socks. I soon met at the local men as various as the huge Irishman with the proportions of a prize fighter who had formerly served as bodyguard to a president of the International Union, and the Trotskyite intellectual complete with turtle-neck sweater and curly pipe. My warmest welcome came from a bearded Moslem, who threw his arms around me, kissed me on the cheek, and informed me that we were all brothers regardless of what we believed. Moslem or Marxist, within the local these men almost always referred to each other as "Brother."

I came to see that the union members stood together when opposing the company management. I also saw conflicts among union politicians erupt into rough-and-tumble, sometimes vicious political infighting. Many of them were experienced production workers who so disliked the assembly line that they were willing to do almost anything to get and keep off it. For them a union job offered a way of escape, with added attractions of power, status, and some increase in income. But since the men seeking this refuge always far exceed the number of union jobs available, political battles were bound to occur.

These come to a climax in elections for officers of the local. In the first election I saw, the area around the local building teemed with people carrying signs, wearing paper hats, and filled with excitement. Cars regularly arrived and disgorged voters who ran the gauntlet of candidates to the voting booths. I worked my way around the polls, stopping to talk with various politicians and collecting the slates of candidates each group was handing out.

Jamie Sparks and Bob McCormick were the first I met. They
wer glad-handling all they could reach and promising that they
could run the local better than Leblanc. Both seemed very happy
to talk to me and told me a lot about how the election worked.

I found Larry standing in front of the local, not glad-handing
so much as just watching. He said I had missed the real excitement. Early that morning there had been a fistfight between two
old political enemies, one white and the other Negro. Their argument in front of the polls turned nasty, and when one candidate
could no longer stand the taunts of the other he hit him, knocked
his teeth out, and pitched him to the ground, gashing the back
of his head. The victim was taken off to the hospital, and his one-
eyed assailant disappeared. Forbes was disturbed about this fight,
especially because of its racial overtones. "It could mean more
trouble," he said.

I had chatted with Lee Calucci several times in the corridors of
the local, but now, as we talked outside the polls, a long tale
of double-dealing, back-stabbing, and reverse racial discrimination
poured forth. The maneuvers he described sounded endless, but
certain points seemed to stand out. In the first place, Lee has
tried to be a faithful union representative and has gone out of
his way to help the men with their problems. He has served fairly
and without racial discrimination in an area of the plant which
is 90 per cent Negro. Second, in this election certain ambitious
Negro union politicians had directed a thoroughly racist campaign
to destroy him politically because they wanted his job. Finally,
in the course of the campaign those who were trying to destroy
him were making a big show of being his devoted friends.

I don't suppose that Lee was ever entirely unrealistic, but in
this case, when he had tried to help his fellow workers and they
made every effort to destroy him as a result, a sense of the vicious-
ness of human nature broke in upon him with a force that shook
him.

"I'm not going out of my way to help those guys any more,"

he said. "I'm going to run for union office now, not to help anybody, but because it's a good job, and without it I'd be out of work because I don't have enough seniority."

Later I had a cup of coffee with a union official and his wife. He seemed tired and fed up.

"I've done a good job," he said. "Why should I also have to stand around and smile and shake hands and play the nice guy?" His opponent, he claimed, was not only an inactive union member but also a nigger-hater. He further complained that the local administration was running a lily-white slate for the first time in years.

But many seemed to find union politics an exhilarating test of wit. I heard a few weeks later that one generally responsible and reasonable official stood outside the polls on election day and asked the voters as they came whom they would vote for. If the voter mentioned his opponent, he would say, "Good. He's a fine man, but vote for me too, won't you? He's running for the day shift. I'm running for the night shift."

In trying to follow this suggestion, the confused voter would void his ballot and thus deprive his own candidate of another vote.

The same man's backers were reported to have thoughtfully offered to drive some of his rival's supporters to the polls, only to take them a couple of miles in the opposite direction and let them out in a field.

"Now you've seen how democracy works," a new friend said with a grin as I prepared to leave for home. Since a certain political diffidence and regard for moral uprightness were fed to me with my Yankee mother's milk, this display of democracy should have appalled me. It did; but I also found it strangely refreshing. For here were men who knew what they wanted and were willing to fight for it without any display of middle-class mock-modesty.

FINDING A FOOTHOLD

If my reactions to the local were mixed, so were those of the local to me. In the beginning my presence was bound to cause embarrassment and confusion and arouse suspicions and hostility. The problem lay less in my unexceptional physical appearance than in my mildly intellectual New England demeanor and clerical collar. The first time I attended a meeting, for instance, a little Italian sidled up, pressed a five-dollar bill into my hand, and said, "Father, will you pray for me?"

At a beer party given by a union group a few weeks later, a union member reeled toward me, saying thickly, "Father, I wish you'd go home. You're just the kind of person I came here to get away from."

At other times overchurched Catholics would eagerly report to me that they offered themselves as chauffeurs to nuns at the neighboring convent on weekends. Many Protestants studiously avoided any extended conversation with me. Some Catholics in bad standing refused to talk to me at all. The greatest embarrassment resulted, comically, when men realized I had heard them use a swearword. "I'm sorry, Father," they would say, "I forgot you were listening."

Such confusion and awkwardness on both sides soon led me to leave behind my clerical garb and appear at the local in a necktie. Probably not the abandonment of clerical clothes, however, but mere persistence led to my gradual acceptance by members of the local. By attending dozens of union meetings, making myself available to talk about local affairs in the corridor before and after meetings, and dropping in to see certain men at their homes in the evening, I soon became a familiar figure to all and a friend to some.

One evening I paid a visit to a Negro worker with whom I had become acquainted at the local. He was cordial but obviously bewildered and a little suspicious of my show of friendship.

"Why are you, a man of the cloth, interested in a bunch of left-wingers like us?" he asked. I told him that I was not particularly interested in left-wingers, but in anyone who wanted to think and talk with me about the human and social problems of industry. And since God is not just concerned about religion, but about the lives of men in all their dimensions, I thought these were good things for a Christian minister to discuss.

He responded in a surprised tone of voice, "You seem to agree with Voltaire that God is love." But then he pressed on with some urgency. "Listen," he said, "I think you and I might be friends. But before you come to my house again, before you sit on my chairs and drink my beer, I want you to understand what kind of a man I am. I call myself a socialist—a kind of screwed-up socialist. And as I understand it Christianity and socialism are incompatible. Do your superiors in the church know you're friendly with socialists? Besides, I'm an agnostic. I didn't tell you before, but I used to be an elder in the Presbyterian Church. When I told the pastor I was an agnostic, he suggested that I resign. I can't understand why you, a minister, would have a man like me as one of your friends."

Then the questions came so thick and fast I could hardly answer them:

"Have you ever really known poverty? I mean the kind that drives women to prostitution and makes men lie and cheat and steal?"

"Have you ever been in a civil rights fight?"

"Why are you so interested in the working class, anyway?"

"Have you ever read *Generation of Vipers?* Would your church let you read a book like that?" Such was one verbal expression of the perplexity, suspicion, and longing I sensed in many of the men, to which they could only rarely give utterance.

Sometimes, however, they took the initiative and offered me an invitation. Bob Keeney, one of the union stewards, suggested that I spend the day with him as he made his rounds in the plant.

His reputation in the local was not one for sterling character: "shameless," "irresponsible," and "unreliable" were words I had heard used to describe him. But I found that wherever we went in the plant Keeney was well known and enthusiastically greeted. Like the proverbial Irish politician, he combined the role of fixer and priest in the intricate tangle of personal relationships and obligations that make up the plant community.

We talked to his constituents wherever we found them, next to their machines, in lunchrooms, or standing outside in the road. Two of them needed to have him explain the benefits possible through their accident insurance and workmen's compensation. He had helped two others whose sons were in trouble with the police: one, convicted of armed robbery, had served his prison sentence; the other had just finished his time for stealing dope from a doctor's office. These and others, with other problems, had secured jobs through Keeney's intervention with the employment office. Keeney's kind of ministry seemed to me so good and important that, if the union did nothing more than make it possible, it was serving society well.

But I was interested to realize that he helped individuals while accepting society without question as it was. "At home men act like men, but at work they act like children," he remarked. I expected his comment to be topped with a dash of social criticism. Instead he continued, "That's why I'm careful not to visit my constituents too often, so that they don't take me for granted and stop listening to my advice."

When another steward at the local described in some detail the nature of his work, I blurted out, "Why, Fred, your job's like mine! Do you ever think of yourself as a minister?"

"Well, no," he replied. "But I see what you mean. But you know, I have to do things no Christian minister ever ought to do. Politics is a dirty game anyhow and union politics is the dirtiest kind. We have some Negro ministers who work in the plant. They understand that and generally steer clear of involvement in union activities. I'm strictly honest with the membership, but you just can't be honest with union politicians. A lot of those guys won't stop at anything to get your shirt. The only way you can stay alive is by keeping one jump ahead of 'em and lying when you have to."

"Perhaps," I suggested, "in some cases lying is the lesser of two evils."

"That's so," he said, "but it's still wrong to do what the Good Book says not to—"

This comment points to the underlying sense of guilt which my presence seemed often to bring to the surface. In many cases, as a personal relationship grew I became more of a friend in their eyes and less of a judge. But never, even after years of regular visits, was my presence entirely free of a certain feeling of unease.

The Chasm

After an interview, the local union president walked with me into the front hall of the local.

"Hey, Elmer," he shouted as he spotted a union member lounging at the doorway, "come over here. There's someone here you should meet." And speaking loudly so that Elmer could hear, he said, "Reverend Paradise, Elmer is one of the worst living characters we have around here. He's a real sinner first class. If you could convert him, you'd really be doing something. I almost think sometimes he's beyond hope." And then as we reached him he said warmly, "Elmer, this is Reverend Paradise. I've asked him to see if he could convert you. I really hope you'll spend some time with him and listen to what he says, because he might even get you to repent and start going to church." Poor Elmer's normally florid face turned a few shades deeper as he muttered something about having to go somewhere very important and shuffled out the door.

This game that was played so monotonously often produced

more embarrassment than laughter. And though it was an inevitable form of kidding, the embarrassment of the victims embarrassed me. I wished the pranksters would stop.

Not embarrassment but dismay overwhelmed me when I met another response which became fairly familiar. In the cafeteria line at a union conference on unemployment, I chatted with an official whom I had seen and spoken to at meetings at the local for the past two years. By the time we reached the end of the line, my questions had led him to begin explaining the methods of shift work in his plant. But when I suggested sitting together so as to talk further, he ignored the overture and quickly took his tray to a table where there was only one seat left, which he occupied. Reactions of this sort made me feel sometimes as if I had a contagious disease. On other occasions, meeting people for the first time in the industrial setting, I was treated almost as a wild animal escaped from the zoo—perhaps not a lion, but possibly a giraffe or a zebra. Not dangerous, but awkward. At times I felt I was regarded as something like a lunatic wandering from a mental hospital. I was treated gently and humored, lest I break out into some kind of bizarre behavior.

The intense discomfort sometimes caused by my presence expressed better than words can the yawning chasm between the world of the church and the world of industry. Being a clergyman, I belonged in the world of the church. My entry into offices and union halls put me on the side of the chasm where I did not belong. Men naturally found this disturbing and puzzling, for I introduced a religious element where it seemed entirely inappropriate.

This gulf between two worlds derived partly from the very structure of American society, which divides work from residence. Just as churches are mainly located in the neighborhoods where people live, so they are almost entirely absent from the industrial institutions in which men work. I saw this vividly from the front doorstep of my home in Detroit. Of the thousands of men who poured from the gate of the large plant virtually across the street each afternoon, only two lived in my neighborhood. Except for these two, I alone among my neighbors had ever been through those gates, which sealed off the industrial complex from my residential community as effectively as the Berlin wall.

Many of the men I met at every level in industry apparently assumed, not only that a clergyman should properly spend his time in his church and residential neighborhood, and must therefore always be ignorant of the real nature of industrial life, but also that he represented a world view incongruous with that of industry. Some with tender consciences saw the incongruity of standards on opposite sides of the chasm in terms of moral conflict. A salesman reflected this sense of turmoil when he confessed, "I want to be a good Christian, and I feel I succeed from the time I come home at night till I make my first call in the morning. But my job makes all kinds of demands that I do things a Christian shouldn't do. For instance, my boss takes it for granted that I distribute whiskey, football tickets, and hundred-dollar pen-and-pencil desk sets in order to keep business. Of course I don't have to do what he says—if I don't mind not eating."

More typical, perhaps, was the man who saw no conflict because he accepted the separation as good. "In different games you play with different rules," he said. "At home and at church you play with one set of rules, and in business you play with another. You just have to be sure you know what field you're playing on at any particular time. Almost everybody who's been a success at building up a business has to play dirty once in a while, if you see it in terms of the family and the church. But by the rules of business he might have been quite aboveboard in what he did."

On the industrial side of the chasm, with its absorption in matters relating to production, efficiency, or the union contract, questions about the church or religious faith seem entirely foreign. Indeed, for those whose minds had been really shaped by in-

dustrial categories of thought, religious faith was largely unintelligible.

For those, on the other hand, who in private life felt they
could understand and accept religion, it offered few insights into
life in industry. These men, I found, characteristically denied God
in the world of their industrial involvement, not with any jaw-
clenching rejection, but with an indifferent shrug. Through the
years, it is true, clergymen have preached "industrially relevant"
sermons, conferences have been run on Christianity and economic
life, articles and books have appeared on religion and business,
and in a few instances pastors have carried on counseling programs
in factories in the employ of the management. For the men I
met, all these efforts of the churches had been unable to show
that their faith and teachings were worthy of industry's serious
consideration.

These men might be able to understand Christian theology—
they might even find it possible to believe in God—but at work
they ignored religion because it made no difference. Through the
years knights of the faith have sometimes ridden forth to find
and kill the dragon Unfaith in his industrial den. But after they
exhaust themselves charging at the giant beast, Unfaith instead
finally overcomes them, not by the sharpness of his teeth and
claws but by the crushing weight of his impregnable indifference.

I had become a minister convinced that the Christian faith was
both true and urgently important. Venturing from the church
across the chasm into the world of industry I found myself shaken
by an environment in which most men assumed its total ir-
relevance. The force of my obsessive inquiry—"How can industrial
man find the Christian faith to be significant?"—may have been
an amplification of my own inner question: "How can I believe?"
For me it had to be answered in industry, for here vast numbers
of men spend their best energies, here the shape of American
culture is being determined, and here the question arises in its

most acute form. In another connection a Detroit manager once said in an address, "We and our families tend to think of ourselves in relation to our employment even more than we think of ourselves as part of a residential community. Moving from place to place as we frequently do, we do not put down roots in the community, but take the corporation as the principal institution to which we attach ourselves." If the Christian faith is to speak to the heart of industrial man (I reasoned), it must confront him in the world of his work.

I continued, therefore, to make what seemed like the most fruitful approaches to all three phases of the industrial scene: the unions, the managers, and the workers themselves, and back of the three, the church parishes of which many of them were members. Although the realms of labor and management were very different (for the sake of coherence the latter is considered separately in Chapters Four and Five below), the reception I found in both places was much the same. In both, many men were too preoccupied or defensive to give me much time.

For instance, after a meeting with a company education director, he said kindly as we walked toward the door, "We're not against spiritual values, you understand—we're just too busy to think about them. We just don't feel they're very important."

A manager said, "I can see how the industrial mission proposes to help the church, but I can't see how it's going to contribute anything to my company. Unless it does, we're not justified in spending company time on it."

"I don't understand your objectives," a union official complained. "What do you expect to come out of your discussions concretely? What is your long-range program? Are you going to present a policy document to the chairman of the board?"

My frustration increased when I was told, "I really don't see what Christianity has to offer beyond what the best industrial consultants are saying today. In my opinion they are already teaching an approach to management very much in accordance with the teachings of Christianity."

Yet I couldn't be angry when a man exclaimed, "Talk honestly with you? You're crazy! I can't even let the guy in the next office know what I'm thinking. This is a competitive business, and I'm not planning to get squeezed out!"

In the first year the battering of such rebuffs made my ego sensitive and raw. Occasionally, and almost as bad, I was accepted as a potential unpaid public relations man who could be used. Union leaders were tempted to regard me as an enemy who might be won over, and managers as one of their own who might possibly betray them, but in both camps were men who felt it worthwhile to subject me to snow jobs designed to impress me favorably with their own organization.

I endured this treatment when necessary, protested it when possible, and continued my search. Some of the men seemed in a way flattered by my interest in them. Others seemed to welcome the sort of reassurance my friendship offered. But best of all, I discovered men who were intrigued by my interest in the human issues in industrial life. I was looking for men like these and found they were not rare. With them I made a start.

Detroit Industrial Mission

The industrial mission offered a strategy and a means to pursue this quest. Like any mission work, it involved three tasks.

1. The mission must make contact with and engage the mission field. For us in Detroit this meant winning trust, making friends, and keeping in regular contact with men in industry. It meant finding means to start an ongoing conversation with men at or near their place of work.

2. The mission must learn how to translate and interpret the gospel in a way meaningful to the culture of the mission field.

This meant, first of all, immersing ourselves in the world of industry, to listen and learn and become as much a part of the culture of the factory as possible, and then try tentatively to find points of contact between the experience and thinking of men in industry and the religious tradition.

3. The mission must develop indigenous organization within or close to industrial institutions. For us, this meant finding ways to create groups of men in industry eager both to pursue the quest for an industrial expression of their religious faith and to develop a quality of life within industry consistent with it. Such organizations have traditionally been called missionary churches.

Our initial hopes that local parishes could be used as bases from which to engage Detroit's industrial corporations gradually gave way to the conviction that we would have to leave them and the whole world of residence behind and start afresh, after a leap across the abyss into the enclosed, isolated world of industry itself. This belief grew partly out of our experience working in the parishes (described in Chapter Six) and partly out of our sense that the gulf is so wide and the worlds on either side of it so different that words heard in churches on the residential side simply cannot be carried over to the industrial scene.

A man I met on the industrial relations staff in an assembly plant vividly illustrates the deadening effect of this separation. He has traveled widely in Europe and spends every vacation at the famous French Protestant religious community at Taizé. There a diet of reading, prayer, and conversation with the brothers has made him both convinced and enthusiastic about their brand of Christianity and its worldly implications.

"How much do your work associates know about this interest of yours?" I asked.

"A few of them know enough to kid me about it once in a while, but not enough to begin to understand it. I don't feel I know anyone at work with whom I could talk about it openly," he answered.

This situation puts the Church in a predicament not unlike that of the labor movement in the 1930's. The American Federation of Labor was originally organized along craft lines. Members of the same craft belonged to the same union and organized locals in their residential neighborhoods. Thus in a single local one could often find men with jobs in a great variety of places. In one plant it was possible also to find workers eligible for membership in several unions and many locals. But this old and powerful organization failed in every attempt to unionize the workers in the big factories of the basic industries of the country. Some became convinced that the only way to organize these big plants was to develop unions with a different structure, which would parallel the structure of the industries rather than reflecting craft divisions. The AFL, bound by its tradition, opposed this new kind of development within the labor movement. The result was a revolt and the birth of an independent labor group, the Congress of Industrial Organizations. Thus only the CIO, with its industrially structured unions, succeeded in organizing the basic manufacturing industries.

Parish church organization is like the AFL: it is an old and powerful kind of ecclesiastical institution. But we came to feel that it might be simply unfitted by its very structure to engage the big industrial complexes of our society. What was needed was an ecclesiastical CIO. To say this is not to attack the parish, any more than to say that a hen cannot swim like a duck is to attack the form and value of hens.

Unlike the CIO, we were determined to engage men at every level of corporation life. We disagreed with the Marxists, who told us our time was wasted in talking with managers; and we disagreed in turn with those who argued that managers alone had power to make the time spent with them significant. The friends we already had in the industrial settings we had chosen seemed to offer a natural place to begin. And we knew very well that making the leap involved danger of falling into the chasm ourselves and becoming outsiders in church and industry alike, with little psychological support from either.

The strategy of mission, then, demanded the building of communication out of which might come a new understanding of religious faith appropriate for industrial life. Unlike some traditional missionaries to foreign lands, for us preaching was unthinkable as a way to begin. We sensed from our first contacts that in industry we were entirely without authority. As representing an institution which is in some sense powerful, we were met with respect. But as outsiders, ignorant of industry, we were listened to with indifference if not contempt. In his *Point of View*, Kierkegaard wrote on this point of mission strategy that

. . . in a "Christian" country, thousands of people live under the monstrous illusion that they can be Christians as a matter of course, and live at the same time in categories quite foreign to Christianity. If a religious writer seeks to dispel this illusion or a missionary seeks to reintroduce Christianity into Christendom, he must not attack the illusion directly. A direct attack only strengthens a person in his illusion, and at the same time embitters him. There is nothing that requires such gentle handling as an illusion, if one wishes to dispel it. But rather the missionary must first of all find his man where he is and begin there. In order to help a man effectively, I must understand what he understands and understand more than he understands. But the helper must humble himself, be patient, and prove to be a good listener. Let him know that you understand what he understands as he understands it.

A missionary in Christendom will always look rather different from a missionary to the heathen. The missionary must adapt himself to the mood of his hearer (all things to all men). He must not be overanxious and on his own behalf to be regarded as religious. He must not be too concerned about what the so-called Christians think of him. Even if a man will not follow where one endeavors to lead him, at least one can compel him to take notice.*

Earning the right to be heard by humbly listening until we

* This passage extracted from my Journal is my summary of Kierkegaard's argument on pp. 22–36 of *The Point of View*, translated by Walter Lowrie (London: Oxford University Press, 1939).

could prove we understood our friends was at least as important
for us in Detroit as for Kierkegaard in Denmark.

For Kierkegaard, however, the cloak of humble listening hid
an underlying theological clarity. For us, listening was easy; in-
experience made us humble. We were in the unenviable position
of a salesman who meets prospective customers without quite
knowing the present form of the commodities he is hoping to
sell. We were only certain that traditional theology and ethics
would not do. Evidence piled up that as far as these men were
concerned traditional theological formulations roused neither
comprehension nor interest, while most critiques of industry on
the basis of Christian ethics seemed out of date. For example,
the power of the labor unions and the comparative affluence of
Detroit's industrial workers muted the traditional Christian arguments for social justice. The diminishing number of outrageous
labor relations practices made Christian pleas for industrial democracy of the style of the 1930's or earlier fall on entirely indifferent ears. In spite of our name we found we brought to
industry no peculiarly Christian answers. Instead we brought a
concern, a question, and an invitation for men to join with us
in an exploration. In partnership with the men we came to know,
we hoped to wrest from the raw materials of their experience a
new and relevant understanding of Christian faith and ethics. We
hoped to rescue the word theology and its substance from the
musty studies of eccentric scholars, where in popular imagination
it lay imprisoned. For us theology would mean quarrying, out
of the best of our religious tradition, insights with a critical bearing on life in industry. We expected that most of the time we
would not be using religious terms or engaging in pious exercises,
and we looked for men of all faiths and no faith at all to join
us in asking, "What is the significance of industrial work?" and
"How can we find freedom and grow to maturity within the
plant community?" and "How can we balance our responsibilities

to our superiors, our subordinates, the company, our family, and the community?"

In wrestling with such questions as these we believed we were approaching the heart of authentic theological concern. We knew that theology would not offer specific solutions to concrete industrial problems, but we insisted that it could reveal purposes and meanings which would make a difference. Here we met the charge that our concerns could be better pursued by the American Management Association or the Harvard Business School. But unlike these organizations, our purpose was not primarily to produce more efficient managers, more productive workers, and more profitable corporations, but rather to discover a new and industrially appropriate way of being Christian, and the means to move industrial organizations to better advance the cause of man. This would involve helping men not only to think more profoundly about the industrial issues they were already grappling with, but also to consider questions that had not yet occurred to them, which are seemingly distant from the details of their jobs.

Since from the beginning our strategy aimed at developing a large number of groups in industry, we recognized informative and interesting lunchtime discussion with individuals as merely the first step. Through it we began our dialogue by learning as much as we could about the life and people inside the walls of industrial plants. Through it we also found men who were willing to gather their colleagues or workmates to meet with us for group discussion series. The membership in these discussions came voluntarily, each group drawn from men at more or less the same level in the corporate hierarchy, and met usually at the place of work.

We encouraged managers as much as possible to devise curricula for themselves, chair their own meetings, and reserve for us the role of a resource. With workers in the plants we operated more informally: the worker who gathered his friends at work for a lunchtime discussion would expect us to provoke response by a brief statement of some current controversial theme. We considered these shop floor discussions most successful if they ignited intense and hilarious argument, and hoped that at least some of these groups would develop their own sense of identity, a common commitment, and momentum and leadership. We had dreams that they might generate the kind of enthusiasm that would lead both to the spontaneous multiplication of groups and to industrially relevant action.

No doubt these great aspirations on the one hand and our puny staff and shoestring budget on the other presented a ridiculous contrast. We knew our dreams might prove to be mere fantasies.

We knew also that John Wesley worked intensively in England for twenty years before Methodism suddenly took shape as a dynamic movement.

We remembered the mustard seed.

TWO

♦ ♦

Getting Acquainted

ALTHOUGH MY PLUNGE into the world of labor began in union halls and offices, from the start I hoped to learn to know the Detroit workers in the plants themselves which were their native industrial haunts. My plan was to make the acquaintance of individuals and casual groups of men, and if possible to meet regularly for discussion with a number of such groups, where I could win a standing invitation; also with the help of shop stewards or other workers perhaps to convene some new groups as well. I hoped to find that this pattern, developed by the industrial mission in Sheffield, England, would prove viable in Detroit. But while our relationships in the union locals multiplied and group discussions with managers were progressing, our requests for regular access to shop floors met with a series of disappointing rebuffs from management of big companies.

Only after two and a half years, when we found a small company president relaxed enough to open the gates, were we allowed through. An official from union headquarters offered to take me in, this first time, and introduce me around. As we walked from shop to shop, I found the blinding brightness of welding torches, the thump and whine of machines, and the ear-splitting staccato of riveting immensely stimulating. I sensed that both of us were anxious about the reception I would have, for he muttered nervously as we went about the terrible working conditions. When we met the chief steward in his office and a small group of men in the time office, he chattered and joked about wanting to take up the collection in any meeting we would have.

The chief steward went off to his Bible study group as soon as the whistle blew for lunch, and my guide, with a steward named Doc, took me around. As I expected, we found that at lunchtime the workers left their jobs and gathered in little knots sitting along the wall, in corners next to the machines, or in the nooks and crannies that honeycomb most plants. On this first day we had time during the lunch break to meet three groups. I was introduced, and said I wanted to learn about life in the plant and to discuss many subjects with them so that I could give ministers of the church a true picture of what goes on. As examples I mentioned Sunday work, union racketeering, and unemployment. Then I asked what they thought of this idea and whether I might come and visit them at lunchtime again. I was delighted to find a positive response in each group, and as I gave my examples they seemed quite ready to launch into discussion of all of them. As among the English workers, in each group one person disagreed with every point I made about industry, while another wanted to argue that in the plant the law of the jungle rules.

When the whistle blew for work to start again, Doc took me around the plant and introduced me to a number of workers and foremen. At first the workers seemed uncomfortable in the presence of a minister, and Doc did not put them more at ease when he suggested that they have a little gathering with me. In contrast to the Sheffield works, here Baptists abounded. Their presence seemed to intensify rather than allay the fears of the rest about things of the church. But the door had finally opened.

Two weeks later I brought a sandwich into the plant at lunchtime and sat down with one of the groups. Their welcome led to a general discussion about conditions in the shop, which I contrasted with those in the Sheffield steel works. This talk proved interesting enough so that they responded warmly to my offer to return, which I did three weeks later. Meanwhile, the next week I came unannounced, intending to try the same thing with the other two groups I had met on the first visit—only to discover that layoffs and transfers had dissolved them both. I did find Doc, however, and we sat together munching sandwiches.

"What do the men generally talk about during lunch hour?" I asked him.

"I'd hate to tell you," he replied with something like embarrassment. "They sometimes describe everything they did the night before." He added quickly that one group often talked about hunting and fishing and another about leaving the plant and starting a business.

"They don't say much about the news, or even TV programs," he said. It looked to me as if my job might be to stimulate the men to venture upon subjects they didn't usually discuss together.

"Would you like me to get some of these guys together next time you come?" Doc asked.

But neither Doc nor I knew how difficult it was going to be to convene a group. His first attempt was hindered by layoffs which resulted in a reduction of the number of men working in his shop. Of those left he could only persuade two to sit down with us. Nick, another worker, assured us we could do better in the frame shop. On the appointed day, when Doc and I found him he was eating alone. Eventually two men joined us who had promised Nick they would come. Meanwhile Doc and I walked around to invite some of the men he knew to enlarge the circle.

From one group we approached the response came, "We don't want to be bothered."

From another the answer came back, "If he sits down here, I'm leaving."

Then when Nick tried to introduce me to one of his friends, the latter ignored me completely and glared at him, growling, "I don't know your language. I can't understand a word you say." And he turned and slouched off.

As I entered the plant on my next visit I still had hopes that Doc could convene half a dozen men for a group discussion. I had phoned him the night before and he had assured me that he would gather a group together for me at noontime. I discovered he was not in his usual place, and a worker told me that he was at the other end of the shop, where I found him busily making chalk marks on the floor.

"Oh, I forgot you were coming," he said. "Please forgive me! I just got permission from the foreman today to build a boat trailer for myself here in the shop. I haven't thought about anything else all morning."

In reply to my question he responded, "No, I haven't even time to come and sit in on a discussion, let alone convene one."

Giving up on Doc for the day, I went to one of the small groups with whom I had talked before; as soon as I joined them the leader said Doc had asked him to come and help him. So the whole group and I stood around and "helped" Doc start to build his trailer.

The idea began to penetrate my consciousness that, in spite of their willingness, neither Nick nor Doc had sufficient force of personality or respect from the men to draw together a group to meet with me. If I was going to have group discussions in the plant I needed to find a leader. Gaunt, big-nosed Pinky Aldrich proved to be such a man. He had helped organize the local originally, had held a variety of union offices, and had the respect of both management and men. One night I dropped in at his house and found him to be the father of eight children and owner of a boat and a much-used fishing rod. As we talked we found ourselves drawn to each other, and by the end of the evening he had agreed to try to bring together some of his friends for regular lunchtime discussions with me. The next day seven of us met, and Pinky urged me to tell about my experiences in English industry. A group was born.

In the meantime I had lunched periodically with the group I had met on my first visit. They expressed little interest in either politics or current affairs, and really did not seem to like to talk much. I knew I would have to strike a spark somehow if our conversations were not to be smothered by stodginess. A new man who joined the group by chance became the steel my flint needed. I steered the discussion to the topic of honesty.

"Should you tell a dying man he has cancer?" I asked as provocatively as possible.

"Do we have a right to fool our wives about the size of our income?"

"Can we be honest in collective bargaining?"

In the discussion that followed the new member acted as straight man, asking the right questions at just the right time, venturing outrageous opinions, and breaking down the reserve of the whole group. With him participating, it not only continued to meet but enlarged its membership as men drifted over from other parts of the shop, drawn by the sound of laughter.

Gradually I began to extend my contacts throughout the company until, after an election, the new local president took me on a tour to show me the overall geography of the firm. I realized with immense satisfaction that I was becoming acquainted with men all over the plant. I attended meetings at the local, visited men at home, talked with them individually in the plant, and soon was meeting regularly with six different groups of workers.

Contact continued with about that number of groups from this plant for the next four years.

On a typical visit I spent the lunch hour in a group discussion and during the afternoon engaged in serious conversation with perhaps ten workers individually and had numerous brief encounters with others. Through free access to this plant, I was thus able to have significant contact with more people in industry in a day than had been possible without it in a week. When, soon after, a large corporation offered similar access to one of their plants, the sheer quantity of my relationships almost doubled, and I was seeing a dozen groups in regular rotation.

In these encounters I was amazed at how quickly strangers sometimes opened up to me. Once, almost immediately upon our casual meeting, a Negro worker I was not sure I had met before began sharing his family and vocational predicament. "I've been to college and I'm working at a job like this," he said. "My boy—he's eight years old—still thinks that someday he might be the President of the United States. And I don't know how to tell him that because of the color of his skin, he never can be."

I had not talked with an old Scotsman many times before he said, with hesitation but very seriously, "Do you mind if I tell you something personal?"

"Why, no."

"You really should pay a little more attention to your grooming when you come in here. The men would listen to you more carefully if you did. Why, I could hardly believe you were a minister myself when I first met you! You should always have your pants pressed and your shoes shined and not run down at the heels. And you should have your hair cut more often and keep it combed. And look, you're wearing a blue shirt. A white shirt costs no more and it makes you look so much more dressed. Take note of what I say, Reverend, for you deserve to be listened to. You've had a good education."

Yet I was discouraged at the impenetrable wall of suspicion and distance that stood between me and some of the men. One group I had met with twice, and arranged with Jimmy, the convener, to meet a third time. As I approached, a man rose and strode off in the opposite direction. Jimmy stepped out of the group to speak to me. I winced at his words and five minutes later was on the phone to the chief steward.

"Jimmy's been telling me they've decided in spite of all he can say that I'm a management spy. That time, the month before last, when I asked them about company attitudes made them suspicious. He says their minds are made up: they don't want to talk to me."

The steward laughed. "Now you see what we go through here in the union office. There's always some rumor going around that has no foundation but gets people all stirred up. And they come into the office blowing their top, and nothing you say will convince them."

ISSUES AND ATTITUDES

Yet in the course of hundreds of individual conversations and group discussions, I began to know workers well and discovered them to be, typically, very different from the full-time union officials who emerged from their ranks. Unlike their leaders, few workers regularly attended union meetings. Most of them displayed little interest in politics and on many issues seemed more conservative than their union representatives. One of the liveliest groups revealed a fascination for the subject of wealth and the wealthy. One man had read a biography of Henry Kaiser, while another knew a good deal about Joseph Kennedy. They compared the ability, power, and way of life of these rich men with their own. Although they expressed some resentment at the privileges of the rich and their supposed exploitation of the poor, in these workers' minds the Henry Kaisers and Joe Kennedys of the world were more heroes than villains. And unlike their union leaders, this particular group preferred a sales tax to an income tax, complained about inflation, argued for the reduction of government spending instead of a tax increase, and complained that the government wasted too much money.

On another day I asked how they felt about integration. Only one man in the group was from the South, and they all made it clear that they had nothing against Negroes. In fact, they bragged about their readiness to work with them in the plant. But they did not want them in their neighborhoods, in their homes, or as personal friends.

"If God had meant us to mix like that he wouldn't have made separate races," one worker explained. Another stressed the loss of value to his property if Negroes were to move into the neighborhood.

"Sure I work with them," another said, "but while I'm here it's as if I was dead. I don't have any choice. The minute I go out those gates it's different."

They admitted that Negroes and whites sat in separate groups at lunchtime. Even in the plant they would not mix socially on a normal basis. My contention that we should ultimately aim at a thoroughly integrated society led to heated discussion and the charge leveled at me: "You're full of condensed milk!"

The next week as I walked through the shop, Pinky stopped me to say, "I hear you're getting in trouble. Up till now you've got along well with the men. But I hear you're trying to stir up race conflict and weaken the union. In fact, some of the men think that's your whole object in being here. We're proud of our race relations here. We've never had any trouble. We don't mind working with them, but we don't want to have to mix with them at home or outside. If you bring up that subject again and talk the way you have been, you probably won't be welcome here any more."

He advised me to begin my next discussion with the group by assuring them that I was interested in many things besides race, and that I would not bring up the subject again. Since he was probably the most widely respected workman in the plant, his advice was worth listening to. And since I met the group as their guest, on their own ground, I ought not to deliberately offend them. Yet if we were to talk at all, I felt I had to be honest as well as diplomatic.

The next time I met with them I told them so. But as I walked out of the plant that day Pinky's warning words rang in my ears, and my heart felt sore.

In every group I met regularly we eventually discussed our feelings about work. In this plant little of the work involved moving production lines typical of automotive assembly operations. The men custom-made steel girders for large construction projects and fabricated parts for comparatively small numbers of specialized steel vehicles, and assembled them. This reqired everything from skilled electricians and mechanics to rough labor, with the bulk of the workers either operating punching, drilling, or cutting machines or else welding, riveting, or working as unskilled helpers. As the work varied, so did the feelings about it. These were varied and in some cases profoundly ambivalent. Many of the men insisted that they hated their work. "I die every morning when I come through those gates," Nick told me. "And I don't come back to life till I go out again in the afternoon. If you don't believe me, watch the difference in the way we come to work and leave it. Coming we walk steady but not fast. But when the whistle blows at the end of the shift we stampede for the gate. We can't get away from this place fast enough."

Another complained, "Work gets deadly monotonous. You go to the same place day after day, year after year, and do almost the same thing with almost the same people. I think that's why so many guys act goofy. They're just trying to break the monotony. I've heard men carry on a perfectly crazy argument for the longest time, and get real mad in the end. And they know better than that. They're just arguing for the sake of arguing.

"Last week on the way to work I got a ticket for not really stopping at a stop sign. I didn't tell anybody about it, but one of my friends saw it happen and he must have spread the word around the shop. In the first part of the morning six guys came up to me at different times and kidded me about my police record. They must be desperate for something different to do if they have to keep up a thing like that."

I asked him if he did not prefer working in a factory to scratching a living out of the North Carolina hills where he was born. "I'm not really sure," he said. "The main thing about this life is that I'm used to it now."

A few men claimed to like their jobs. Several times I accepted a crane operator's invitation to climb up into his cab and ride with him while he worked. He told me that he fell in love with the crane the first time he operated it. In twelve years his deep affection for it had not diminished. He delighted in showing me the fine points: how he had to be an expert observer of the whole shop and anticipate the next operation for which the crane would be used; how he had learned to sense the subject of conversation on the floor below, even though he could not hear it; how he had learned to operate the controls without thinking or looking at them so as to be able to give full attention to the job on the floor. He even seemed to enjoy telling me how the taciturnity of his nature had been deepened by long hours in the remote crane cab, until his wife complained at his almost complete silence when they had friends in at home.

Another worker surprised me with the claim that his monotonous job on the foundry line gave him a good chance to reflect on "weighty thoughts" culled from his reading. Since I knew he had read widely in Marxist literature and social criticism, I believed him when he insisted that much of the time he was not daydreaming but really thinking.

Whether they hated their work or loved it, what evidence we have indicates that without it many suffer a subtle psychological deprivation. During these years a recession took on such serious proportions that the unions organized a national rally of the unemployed in Washington to rouse Congress and the administration to remedial action. I was invited to go along, and while on the train talked at length with the crowds of laid-off workers. Although a considerable number had been out of work for a year or more and had somehow been able to survive financially, what struck me most was the sense of bewilderment, displacement, and loss of identity they seemed to share. Without places of employment these men found it hard to answer, to themselves, who they were and how they fitted into the life and purpose of the community. Moreover they were—strangely, one might think—objects of moral disapprobation to those who still had jobs. Very commonly, in discussion in the plants, workers condemned the unemployed as lazy and insisted that anyone who really wanted a job could find one.

A unique opportunity came to test these observations. Jesse Christian and Jim Campbell were Presbyterian ministers who had left their congregations to participate in the life of workers for four years on an assembly line and then joined the staff of the Detroit Industrial Mission. Their experience had overwhelmed them with the sense that, in spite of certain exceptions, most workers hated their work.

First, it bored them. They could not see it as a meaningful frame of reference. So far as most of them were aware, work meant simply a pay check.

Second, it gave them no feeling of achievement. For most men it required little or no skill—could be done or left undone, but could not be done better or worse. Personnel office files often reflect this, in the fact that records are kept only of workers' absences, tardiness, and occasions of discipline. The cards have no space for noting down special effort or an exceptional sense of responsibility.

Third, it gave them no sense of significance. Workers were easily replaceable. It mattered little to the process of production if a particular man came to work on a certain day or stayed at home. Working on the assembly line, men found themselves at the lower edge of the working class, living without status or respected identity in American society. Jesse and Jim felt that assembly-line conditions inhibited growth to individual maturity and offered little opportunity to live an authentically Christian life. They found it almost impossible to see how their work or that of their fellows could be seen as service to God.

RELIGION AND THE WORKERS

This does not mean that many of the men were not devoutly Christian. But the question of the quality of their religion—and my own—in the industrial situation shadowed me on every visit to the plants. Sometimes workers themselves would bring up the issue. A devout Lutheran accosted me with the remark that he was shocked every time he heard men swearing in my presence without my expressing disapproval or even raising an eyebrow.

"It isn't right," he said, "that you listen to such un-Christian language without criticizing it."

I tried to point out that we are called to accept men as they are and not always to be trying to reform them. "If swearing was the worst thing these men did, they'd be a lot of saints. Your God is too small, if you think that swearing is one of His major concerns."

Apparently this was a successful witness, in that my reaction caught his attention and shook him a little. But I felt uneasy that a Christian's witness in this place should be over such a trivial issue. I wished it might have been possible to capture his attention rather by behavior revealing a genuine love. This would surely have been a better way to make vivid to his mind the bigness of God. In any case the incident shows how, in spite of my efforts to discard clerical pretensions, I was minutely watched as a representative of the church and an example of Christian living.

When I raised the question of our responsibility in regard to the population explosion with a shop floor group, the men themselves introduced the religious question. Some were Roman Catholics, but only one had more than three children. Nevertheless, the general view expressed was a highly emotional version of the Roman Catholic position on birth control.

"Would you deny life?" one of them said. And another added, "Isn't it better to live for a short time, even if you're hungry, than not to live at all? Anyway the world still has plenty of resources to feed a much bigger population than we have now."

"What right have you to decide that somebody shouldn't be born?" Apparently for these men the ultimate value was human life, quantitatively measured, and regardless of the quality of their lives they felt that the more people there are, the better. Viewed from this perspective the likelihood of world famine had no bearing on the permissibility of birth limitation.

But what interested me most about the subject of birth control as the men saw it was that for the first time, quite naturally and without prompting from me, they began talking about God's purpose and His will.

"Why, if God doesn't want a child to be born, there's nothing you can do to produce him."

"It's for God to decide how many children we have." Here was one area in which God seemed relevant.

When by contrast I deliberately raised the issue of religion with the same group, proposing alternatives to the fundamentalist interpretation of the Bible, I found a strong resistance. I had done it often in England and encountered a lively and positive response.

But in Detroit they said, "Let's not talk about that sort of thing."

"We don't talk about religion."

"We don't know enough about this sort of thing to talk about it."

Perhaps I should have known. Some in the group were Catholic, in good standing or otherwise. Others were Protestants of a rigid if not Pentecostal variety. All felt they should believe in the literal historical truth of the Adam and Eve story. None of them, probably, believed in evolution. They certainly did not feel qualified to challenge the position I took, yet could not accept it without feeling they were betraying what they had been taught. Someone put forth a proof that God did make man out of the dust of the ground, through the claim that science has shown that the elements in the human body are identical with those of the earth. This was to disprove evolution. But in general the whole question was uncomfortable to consider and intolerable to discuss.

Bible discussions did take place at lunchtime. These were study groups led by laymen or ministers who worked in the plant during the week and preached on Sundays. I avoided such groups in an attempt to keep free from the sort of pietism most of them represented. To become identified with this, I felt, would close off any hope of communication with many of the secular types in the plants. Some of my friends and supporters took part in them, however, and occasionally our meetings were at cross-purposes.

"No, tomorrow wouldn't be a good time for you to come down to the plant," Cal Jackson said. "We have our Bible study group meeting every day now, you know. And just now we've gotten to a very exciting point. Horace, our teacher, is going to tell us who the sons of Caleb are that God cursed. The guys are all keyed up to find out the answer, and they wouldn't leave for a discussion with you. I'd leave myself, but I read the verses, and then Horace talks about them, so I can't."

"What else have you been talking about?" I asked.

"Lately he's been telling us how each of the plagues of Egypt corresponds to one of the twelve gods of the Egyptians. He knows so much about the Bible I've never heard of, it's real interesting. He told us about the origin of the races one day. It says God made man out of the dust of the earth. And Horace pointed out that in some places the dust is red, in other places yellow, and black, and white. And so man is different colors in different parts of the world. I never thought of it that way before. But Horace can prove everything he says from Scripture, so no one can win an argument with him."

A whiff of religious opiate came to me with this tale of esoteric escape from reality.

"Do you ever talk about how all this affects your life in the shop?" I inquired.

"No, we don't. We just talk about the Bible."

I went to the plant anyway and met another group without Cal. After lunch I was discussing the difference between Horace's kind of discussion group and mine with one of the most thoughtful and articulate men in the shop.

"I believe we should talk about the Bible only so far as it relates to what we're doing here in the plant," I confessed. "Religion is nothing if it doesn't apply to our lives in the world today. That's why I talk about shop problems and current events and try to look at them from the Bible point of view."

He agreed entirely. "In fact," he said, "I read the Bible for fifteen minutes every morning before I go to work. And there was something I couldn't understand for a long time until I realized it meant the atom bomb."

"What was that?" I asked.

"Vermin pile," he said.*

* ??

THREE

❦ ❦ ❦

LIFE IN THE LOCALS

"THE UNION educational program can be little more than propaganda," explained the education director of the local. He had asked my help in planning a program and already we were at loggerheads on educational philosophy. In our discussion of a prospective speaker he insisted, "It would be just as effective to have him speak to a big group as to a small one. The most we can do is feed these men with information, and it doesn't matter how many people are there listening. I learned more in a class of five hundred at Wayne than in any of the small classes, because the teacher really knew how to put the material over."

"But in a big meeting, isn't it hard to have discussion in which everyone can participate?" I inquired.

"We can't even attempt to get our membership to think for themselves," he replied. "If you give them the whole story and all the facts, it's still harder for them to decide what's right. I think if I myself didn't have so much education, I could make up my mind more easily. We have to feed them slogans. That's the best we can do."

"What do you want the membership to be," I protested, "men or automatons?"

"We can't afford to let them make up their own minds," he insisted. "They might make them up wrong. One fellow from this local saw the TV debate between the union president and a speaker for the AMA. Why, that doctor's position was directly opposed to the man's interests, yet he was more impressed by the doctor than he was by his own president! If we let them have all the arguments, our members may decide against their own interest—and we can't afford that."

This distrust of the workers by union leadership was symptomatic of one of the problems of unions, and one of our problems with them. Among other things, we wanted to improve communication and understanding between groups in industry. But we were confronted by a pervasive obscurantism in certain areas. Another union education director expressed the same distrust of the values of genuine and individual understanding.

"If the shop steward understood management's problems," he said, "perhaps he wouldn't fight so hard for the men."

In spite of this apparent conflict of interest, I gradually won acceptance in a number of union locations. In the course of time I visited more than a dozen locals of two major unions, and their headquarters. This made a small but representative sample of the area's industrial unions. My contacts with friends in these locals were frequent enough, over a long enough period of time, so that I began to appreciate the peculiar ethos of each and to identify the points where one was typical and another unusual. For instance, one contained an influential left-wing group and could usually be counted on to oppose the administration of the International Union. Within another the skilled workers in thirty-odd small tool-and-die shops found shelter. Hillbillies dominated a third.

At first the color and drama of union meetings fed me with a sense of excitement. As this began to pall, I became intrigued by the complexities of the problems under discussion. Finally, personal friendship with the officials themselves warmed and sustained my interest. At two of the locals my attendance was so regular that I practically gained the status of member. Some were membership meetings in which rank-and-file workers participated. Others were executive board meetings attended only by officials. Trying to orient myself amidst the levels and tones of union activity, I realized that I had come on the scene after the original turmoil of organization and after a way of life with company management had been painfully worked out. In some locals union power was still held by the leaders of the first organizing drives. Some militant left-wing leaders so prominent in the forties still survived, but their influence was waning together with the militant spirit of the unions in general. In fact, while I was in Detroit the McClellan Committee hearings and passage of the Landrum-Griffin Act marked the decline of public support and sympathy for organized labor.

The day-to-day business which occupied most of the meetings I attended dealt with detailed problems such as approving new methods of apportioning overtime, the agonizing disputes caused by layoffs, and reports on particularly difficult grievances. Once in a while a routine report would develop into a hilarious debate. Thus a certain Lefty, a dilapidated and vitriolic one-armed worker, in his report on a Christmas party accused other union officers of stealing two thousand popcorn balls.

On one occasion I heard that an executive board member, Otto Lipke, had been charged with drawing expenses from the local, while in the hospital, at the same time he was receiving insurance. At the meeting of the local executive board where this was to be reviewed, I found a large number of observers present, including a row of Otto's political opponents who were sitting around like smirking vultures.

A letter from one of his political enemies was read which made serious allegations concerning his methods of handling union finances, and it was recommended that a committee investigate the matter and report to the board at a future date. This led to a lengthy debate in which Otto was so put on the defensive that he offered to resign that day if it could be shown he had deliberately misused union funds. While the accusing letter was read and discussed, Otto was always referred to as Brother Lipke, and finally, shouting by this time, he affirmed his solidarity with the group by declaring his innocence of being a stooge for The Company.

I dropped in to see him later that week and got a long story of political persecution. He claimed that, unknown to the rank and file, officers of the local were paid their salaries and expenses when sick—so why not lesser union leaders like himself? Moreover, he said, he was the most honest leader in the local and the attack on him was politically inspired.

Sometimes political attacks were pressed with drama and finesse. At a meeting with over a hundred union members present the president raised an issue in which Lipke had been involved.

"I don't want to be critical," the president said, "but in a case like this, never handle it like Lipke did!" By this he clearly implied that Lipke either did not know good union procedure or had deliberately sold one of his constituents down the river. Although it was long past the hour for adjournment, Lipke rose and defended himself vigorously in a forty-five-minute speech. While he spoke, the president stood back smiling blandly. Then before adjourning the meeting, he said quietly to the membership, "Brother Lipke seems to think that the union can't survive without his leadership. Let me remind you it got along well for five years recently when he absented himself from it. (This was a reference to Lipke's removal from union office because of Communist affiliations.) Well, if you think his training has suited

him to lead this local, make him president in the next election.
You can have him!"

Then with a flourish the president produced an earlier issue
of the union newspaper and read a passage from an article written
by Lipke himself, from which one could only conclude that
either then or now he was lying. The excitement of the members
had risen to a high pitch, and at this point they broke out cheer-
ing as the meeting adjourned.

All union political battles were not carried on with such adroit-
ness. Once I arrived late at the regular monthly membership
meeting of a local and found the president so beset by opposition
that he could not keep order or control the meeting. As I found
a seat in the seedy union hall, the opposition's attack on the
treasurer of the local was already under way. Because he had not
been able to prepare his report, due to unforeseen circumstances,
he faced a hail of crude and insulting charges: that he was not
doing his job, that his reports were always late, that he was lazy
and incompetent.

The opposition in this case was numerous enough to cause the
meeting to reject the good reasons and apologies of the treasurer
as well as the administration's other reports. Finally they attacked
the treasurer for giving information to the press about a former
president of the local who had recently been in an accident. (The
newspapers had used the information to discredit the union.) Having made business all but impossible for more than an hour and
a half, the members of the opposition then marched out of the
meeting in a body and left the administration and its supporters
to try to pick up the pieces.

Sometimes the savagery of union politics approached physical
violence. In a predominantly Negro part of a certain plant, threats
of a beating by the leader of the Negro political group frightened
an Italian worker into abandoning his plans to run for union
office. Another Italian politician told me that when he also was

threatened by a fellow worker, he responded, "If you lay a hand
on me, I'll wait my chance, but in the end I'll *kill* you."

"I don't want any killing talk," the other said, backing down.

Political conflict seemed unrestrained by any moral considerations. Those I talked to wished this were not so, but explained
that "this is the way the game's played, and men who can't take
care of themselves shouldn't get involved." Unexpectedly, however, political wounds would often be forgotten when a change
in circumstances made it profitable for enemies to become friends.

The reverse was true in regard to the other perpetual conflict
in union life: the company by its very nature could never become
a friend. But through the years, union and company had worked
out a relationship with a highly developed set of rules involving
as much cooperation as antagonism. Against the corporate enemy
the union leader hurled hostile words, but aimed limited and
ritualized blows. With the political opposition among his union
brothers, he spoke of solidarity but fought with no holds barred.
Only the existence of a "hostile" company, it seemed, made possible the slightest modicum of union solidarity.

In fighting the company the workers felt their power and
dignity. One steward told me how his constituents, watching him
through the glass walls of the manager's office, fiercely criticized
him if they did not see him pound on the table and shout and
swear at the manager. Local and headquarters union leadership
were usually embarrassed when stewards and workers broke the
rules and fought the company in an unauthorized or wildcat strike.
But the authorized strike was the big moment of union strength
against the company. It presented dramatically a massive confrontation between management and union.

At one of these the union was still picketing when I chatted
with the chairman of the local strike committee outside the plant
gates. "You should have been here on Monday morning!" he
exclaimed. "Gee, it was beautiful! You never saw anything like it."

"What was so beautiful?" I asked, wondering vaguely if I had missed a spectacular sunrise.

"Why, we had the place shut up tight! For several hours we stopped all the staff and all the managers from coming in or going out. There wasn't a thing moving anywhere. Gees, it was beautiful!"

Moving Toward Dialogue

During the first few months my attendance at meetings at the local usually involved brief chats with a few people and perhaps a cup of coffee with one or two before the meeting started, and then during the meeting attentive listening from a seat in the hall. My role gradually began to change as I made more friends and became involved in their lives. In one meeting, for instance, almost two-thirds of the time the meeting was in progress I found myself standing in a corridor or a corner of the auditorium in conversation with various friends about current issues under debate, or arranging dates for further discussion at a future time. In a sense I was becoming a personage in the local. A good many knew me as a friend; some discussed union problems with me; on several occasions I was asked to speak at meetings or give an invocation.

This success in engaging the world of labor left me both anxious and frustrated, however. The anxiety sprang from a sense that my achievement was fragile and one false move could shatter the relationship I had so painfully built. On a number of occasions it led me to play it safe when in retrospect I felt I should have been more daring. At one meeting at the local I spoke to the membership about the responsibility of the churches to awaken men's conscience to the problem of unemployment. The chairman then commented that I had disappointed him, because I had not stressed or even mentioned the responsibility of the churches to keep the children of the unemployed out of trouble. At the time I accepted his criticism. On reflection, I realized that I might have urged vigorously that Christianity is not just for children, but has vital importance for grown men and adult society. Another time a union member who belonged to a Trotskyite political group asked me to be sponsor of a left-wing Labor M.P. from Britain. He was coming to discuss nuclear policy at a public meeting. After painful deliberation I declined, on the grounds that I might be thought to believe not only in the M.P.'s right to speak, but also in his personal opinions and those of the Trotskyite group. In later months, when I thought of my timidity on these occasions, I winced.

In some cases I am sure the timidity was mutual that kept either my union friends or me from significant discussion with each other. After an election in which the union administration had engaged in some vicious race-baiting tactics, Jesse and I lunched with one of the union officers. When he denied that any racist tactics had been used, we did not press him. If we had, he might have been persuaded to talk about it, and in that event one of several situations might have emerged:

1. John (the union official) might have said that he believed politics have different moral standards from other areas of life. Or he might think this, but feel he could not admit it because we would not agree with him. If he had said what he thought, at least we could have discussed the issue.

2. He might have confessed that he knew his group was wrong, but was afraid not to go along. Here we might have understood his prudence but strengthened him with a little courage.

3. He might have avowed that he saw no other standard of life and behavior beyond that of union politics. And seeing nothing else, wanted nothing different. Knowing John, I doubt that this was the case, but if it had been, we could have tried to enliven his imagination with other possibilities.

4. He might have revealed that he felt trapped. While hunger-

ing and thirsting after righteousness, he perhaps felt powerless to do anything. In this case we could have suggested resources he had not begun to tap.

In any case, admission would be followed by absolution, so far as any judgment of ours was concerned. But we never got so far. In general, he admitted racial problems in the local, but defensively steered away from any significant discussion of the election and the tactics used to win. One can do little to relieve an area of feeling that has not been articulated. As it was, John hesitated to speak and we hesitated to insist; he was kind to us, we were polite to him, and our lunch conversation was trivial.

Benevolent third parties sometimes tried to prevent genuine encounter in order to protect us. After an evening at a union steward's house talking about my hope of working with certain officials with whom he was associated, his wife phoned the next morning to say that after hearing us talk she was worried about me. "Don't show your whole hand to those people, and don't expect too much of them. They're out for themselves and they'll cut your throat if it'll help them politically. I know some of those men. You can't trust them. They're vicious. But don't let them think you've found them out."

I was touched by her concern, but sensed that to take her attitude would make my work impossible. While being realistic about them I had to like them, too. I had to believe that Christ was in them at least as truly as in a middle-class minister.

Standing between the world of labor and management and between the political factions in the union made me wonder at times whether I could in honesty be a friend with men on all sides at once.

"I don't think you like the labor movement," a worker observed after a discussion with a group of union officials. "There's a lot you don't agree with. You don't agree with us getting forty hours' pay for thirty hours' work, do you? And there's a lot more you don't agree with, isn't there?"

"What makes you think that?" I asked.

"I just watch your face, that's all. Kelly told me to look out for you, that you were some kind of an agent, but I'm fascinated by your technique. You don't express yourself; you encourage everybody else to talk. And you mustn't show your position—that would be a mistake."

"Don't spread it around that I'm antilabor," I begged. "It's not true. I think unions are important, and they need to be strong."

That same week, after the personnel managers' discussion the convener said to me privately, "You know, after the last session one of them said he thought you were pretty prolabor. I think he was still a little suspicious even after I explained how you weren't committed to either side."

My wife said to me, "With all the walking on the razor's edge you do, why aren't you neurotic?"

"Are you sure I'm not?" I responded.

My frustration matched these anxieties. It grew from a sense that, though I listened, learned, and made friends, I had not really opened up a dialogue, nor had I even begun to assemble, or create, a group committed to discussion of the nature of a responsible labor movement and the possible Christian contribution to it. My expressions of interest in establishing informal discussion at the local met with warnings from local leadership that this would be construed by some as political caucusing and threaten my welcome.

THE FORUM

Friends in the local proposed that we meet at my home and offered to help find union members who would participate. Accordingly eleven of us from several locals met one evening in my living room to lay plans for a series of discussions. By the end of the evening we had agreed that we wanted to build our meetings around the social and political issues that face the labor movement. We agreed that we should meet on Saturday evenings every month or two at my house, invite those of our friends in the union who seemed to have an interest in the larger social questions, and each time arrange for a guest to begin the discussion with a presentation. Wives were to be invited, and we would provide coffee, beer, and pretzels.

Nate Weinberg, a United Auto Workers economist, spoke to one of our most successful early meetings. More than twenty people jammed into my living room to hear him expound the effect of foreign economic competition on American labor. In introducing him, I explained briefly the purpose of the meeting and my role in it as a Christian minister.

"If Christianity is understood as being concerned with every aspect of life," I said, "it is not strange but perfectly natural that I convene and chair a meeting of union people to talk about union problems. In fact I consider it my mission in life to bring together groups of men who work in industry to talk about industrial problems as realistically and profoundly as possible."

Nate's presentation gave the facts in a clear and reasonable way, and he handled the mass of questions put to him directly and skillfully. The group found the discussion like a breath of fresh air and continued a vigorous debate of the issues even after he had left. Thinking about the meeting later, I could see in it three main values:

1. The speaker had served as a myth-breaker in demolishing some of the fantastic notions then current in some locals. If our God is the God of truth we were serving Him that evening. Of course, Nate did not have the whole truth, and the facts he presented did not go unchallenged. But he made perfectly clear, for instance, that raising tariffs against foreign foods would not solve our unemployment problems. And in showing the impracticality of the thirty-hour week he provoked one of the union

leaders to say afterward, "He made me feel as if the rug had been pulled right out from under me."

2. The atmosphere in the discussion seemed thoughtful and honest, with good communication within the group. The men seemed open enough to change their minds and relaxed enough to be themselves. A few of those present described it as a new and exhilarating experience.

3. The substance of the discussion could be described as: Who are our neighbors? What are our responsibilities toward them? What is the best way to love them? Although we never became explicitly religious, our discussion of tariffs, international fair labor standards, and foreign aid was full of theological and ethical implications.

Other meetings were successful for quite different reasons. For instance, Jesse Christman talked with the group about work on the assembly line as he had experienced it. Curiously, both his contention that work ought to be a positive and meaningful experience and his proposals for humanizing production-line work evoked sharp debate. At a later meeting Horst Symanowski, a pioneer industrial missioner from Mainz-Kastel, Germany, suggested some radical social goals he thought Christians and union members should support. Both these men brought to the issues such knowledge and freshness that the group had to listen. One evening Malcolm Boyd met with the members to discuss strategy for the civil rights movement. My heart sank when he ignored the stated topic and offered a long, disjointed and subjective autobiographical excursion which began in his childhood and meandered to the present. To my astonishment it became apparent that he had somehow managed to communicate with the group on a subrational level. The discussion that followed proved to be very much on the question of civil rights strategy. Malcolm's plea for integration motivated by love stirred wild controversy.

"We whites must realize that in the world we are a minority," one woman insisted.

"That has nothing to do with it," Malcolm rejoined.

A union leader, his ebony face creased with bitterness, kept muttering, "Give us guns. We've gotta have guns."

And so the discussion raged till, after midnight, the last member of the group, still debating vigorously, stepped out the door. Several told me afterward that this had been one of our best meetings.

In the course of four years the subjects of discussion ranged from automation and the future of work to the Christian response to poverty in America. Among those who provided stimulating fare for the group were Congressman Staebler, Detroit City Councillor Ravitz, Bishop Wickham from England, and the Rev. George Webber from East Harlem.

For me, however, the members of the group themselves were as interesting as the speakers. The discussions attracted a collection of radicals who had given up membership in Marxist associations but preserved their social concern, young committed unionists eager for a chance to discuss the social issues confronting the labor movement, and some older union leaders intent on finding some support and meaning in the organization to which they had given their lives. Altogether, I suspect these types made up only a small minority of union activists. But for them the meetings served a real need. When so much of my work involved taking the initiative and winning only meager support, my surprise was joined by delight when one evening one of the group phoned to urge that we have a meeting of the Forum on the new union contracts just negotiated. And I regretted not having a tape recorder when, during one discussion, group members confessed what the Forum had meant to them. In essence they said that only here had they found a regular chance for serious and open debate of basic principles. In these meetings they had found encouragement to press their efforts for a more socially concerned labor movement. I felt this gave evidence of real success.

For myself also, the group supplied me with some of my closest

friends, glimpses of grace, and opportunities for theological reflection. One man displayed extreme ideological dogmatism and
at the same time proved loyal, forgiving, and appreciative in
situations where I would least expect it. For instance, I took him
to an Industrial Relations Research Association meeting and at
supper he sat next to an industrial manager. He reported afterward that the manager had confided in him that he thought the
workers in his plant deserved as good treatment as the machines.
I was astonished at Bob's approval of this opinion.

"But yes!" he responded to my query. "If we really treated the
workers today as well as we do the machines, we'd be a long way
ahead of where we are now. I was impressed by that manager. I
thought he was great."

Another member of the group had dropped out of college,
joined the labor movement, and after some dramatic experiences
in the east had come to Detroit with his wife ten years before.
They came as members of a small Marxist political party whose
members had been able to cling to the belief that they were there
in the van of history. He went to work in one of the big plants
and participated in the political and industrial activities of his
group until both he and his wife became disillusioned with the
socialist god and quit the party. Although he had great personal
and intellectual gifts and was a sound and effective leader, he
had not achieved any position of great prominence or success in
union politics, but had only managed to survive as a steward. He
had been a promising leader of the workers, expecting to ride
the crest of the new world brought in by socialism. Then it looked
as if he might gain eminence as a respectable union leader. They
had left the home city they loved. They had foregone the joys
of children. He had gone into a kind of industrial work far below
his natural capabilities. All this they had done for the cause of
a revolution that had not come.

"The sacrifice wasn't worth it," they said in the course of a
painfully intense discussion in their kitchen. I tried to say that

the sacrifices they had made were not wasted, that any acts of generosity and human concern are worthwhile. They had done something fine, and to be bitter—cynical in their disillusion—would rob them of the benefits of sacrifice. I was sure that Christianity spoke to their situation, but found I could do no more than affirm the value of their lives as they had already lived them, for I did not know how to use the Christian symbols of the cross and the Resurrection so as to make sense for Marxist atheists.

Yet my conversation with this union steward continued. His involvement in local politics as a member of the opposition resulted, not only in his becoming the target of political attack, but also suffering with the near breakdown of a loyal friend who was subjected to the same pressure.

"It's always the finest people who get bludgeoned," he said to me.

"Yeah," I said, "if Christianity is realistic anywhere, it's in recognizing this."

"That's true," my friend answered. "They did it to Jesus, didn't they? But Billy Budd is the example I always think of."

Without the Resurrection, I thought, we shouldn't think of Jesus any differently than Billy Budd. But I did not know how to talk about the Resurrection to men in industry except to affirm their struggle and suffering to be worthwhile. Maybe this was adequate for the moment. Nevertheless I felt as if most of the modern world was like Mars Hill under Paul's preaching, where the truth of the Resurrection could not be grasped. And yet, another Marxist atheist in the group admitted that while we disagreed with him, Christians were about the only people with whom he could still talk.

We had to admit, however, that in spite of the value we personally found in the Forum, it had insignificant effect on the life of the locals from which its members came. During the period in which we met, at least one local completed the transition from standing out as a place of controversy on social issues and a focus of lively social concern, to suffocating under the dominance of political self-interest and cynicism. Here Machiavelli had triumphed in internal union affairs; for the time being Gompers and his bread-and-butter unionism had come to determine the local's relationship with the company. I saw the writing on the wall as I entered the meeting room just at the breaking up of a leadership meeting of one of the opposition caucuses. I do not know just what happened there, but as I stood around afterward with three friends, their comments showed that they were repulsed and sickened by the kinds of things that had to be done. The chicanery, the demagogy, the betrayal of one's own ideals and convictions, the crude political self-interest, all seemed necessary ingredients in putting together a viable caucus in the local. Some of my friends seemed to be wondering if it was worth it. I had seen a social movement become a self-interested pressure group. Here I felt was a demoralization more serious than the financial dishonesty stressed in the McClellan Committee hearings.

A few of my more idealistic friends voted with their feet and left the labor movement either by going into nonindustrial work or by returning to college. Most of them stayed, because they had no other place to go. I looked around at their faces as they sat in one of the interminable meetings. It was anything but inspiring. Not only were the expressions of the men without any sign of love, joy, enthusiasm, humor, or interest in what was going on, but most of them seemed almost devoid of life. The sagging blankness of Tom's face was hardly enlivened by his simultaneously chewing gum and chomping on a cigar. The only mood revealed by most others was boredom. The scowl on the face of a black nationalist shone forth as a welcome contrast to the forest of zombies around him.

A girl who had fled from East Germany told me once that so great was the distrust among people there, and so frustrating and restricting the life generally, that the people and even her

friends had become "faceless" to her. Some would argue with
a certain amount of justice that the draining away of social
idealism from these union locals merely brings them to the level
of many other institutions in American life. But it saddened me,
since I felt that, by and large, unions not only have performed,
and still perform, a necessary function in our society, but also
stand for certain things to which Christians should be committed:

1. The fact that "we are members one of another." We need
each other. No man is an island unto himself. Alone he is help-
less. "Solidarity Forever" is the theme song, and the emphasis
is that of cooperation for mutual betterment rather than competition for individual gain. Although some ambitious individuals
use the union as a means of individual advancement, and many
look on their union as an organization to get gravy for themselves
personally, this does not destroy the weight of the original affirmation.

2. The fact that man cannot live by bread alone. Although
the unions spend much of their energy in negotiating improved
wages and fringe benefits for their members, the labor movement stands basically for the dignity of man. Perhaps more important for the worker than wage increases is the power the
union gives him to stand up and look his boss straight in the
eye and tell him what he thinks. What the labor movement
needs now is the recognition that its own power needs to be
checked so that, in its zeal to protect the worker's dignity from
affronts by his employer, it does not itself threaten or destroy
that dignity. And further, while the unions defend the individual
worker, they seem today to have no appreciation of the value of
work. It is a question whether a worker himself can have dignity
in his own eyes if he spends his life doing work that seems mean-
ingless.

3. The fact that men are brothers regardless of race, religion,
or national origin. I still get a thrill when I attend a union meeting and find there men of every possible color and appearance

addressing each other as "Brother." Even in the union, as we have seen, this high ideal of human brotherhood is not always accepted in practice. And even more difficult for many union people to recognize is that managers, too, are their brothers. Yet when I left the local, there were still men there who believed in these things.

The dynamic quality of our understanding of mission prevented us from resting with any achievement, but instead focused our attention on newly emerging problems. Nevertheless, within limits, with workers and union leaders we succeeded remarkably. For instance, here we definitely achieved the first goal of mission referred to in Chapter One, which was to build relationship with men in the mission field. And this success was won in the face of many predictions of failure. In goals 2 and 3 of our mission strategy our success was less complete. We failed, of course, to evolve a fully satisfactory interpretation of the Christian faith for labor as well as in developing indigenous groups with their own leadership and momentum. But at certain levels we succeeded in initiating honest theological discussion and probing with workers and union officials for meaning in the religious tradition. Even more clearly than our words, perhaps, our willingness to go to labor on its own ground, to listen carefully and learn about the real problems, and to offer personal friendship—this acted out the central concern of our faith. Because of our work with them many in labor found new understanding and respect for the church. Because of our friendship, some at least were prepared to consider the possible relevance of religion to their lives more seriously than before.

II
THE WORLD OF MANAGEMENT

FOUR

✦ ✦ ✦ ✦

FIRST CONTACTS

COMPARED WITH THE world of labor, entering the world of management should have been easy. Most managers were like myself in having had a middle-class background and education. On Sundays the pews of suburban Episcopal churches groaned with the weight of hundreds who, during the week, occupied the executive offices of Detroit industry. These were some of the first men I met in the city, and their position made it quite possible to telephone them at work and arrange to have lunch with them in a local restaurant or plush company dining room.

But often it proved more difficult than I expected. Some men, in spite of my repeated calls, seemed never to be in or always too busy to return them. Some put me off, explaining that they were much too busy at this time of year. The "Don't call me, I'll call you" kind of brush-off became so familiar to me that I sometimes stared at a phone for minutes at a time before finding the courage to risk rejection by making a call. Others, however—

particularly at the middle management level—seemed happy to talk with me, and through them I grew to appreciate both the reason for the inaccessibility of so many of their colleagues and much about management life in general. Managers near the top, it was explained to me, and those hoping to be on their way up, succeed partly because of their terrific concentration on things absolutely crucial to their careers. Their responsibilities are often so great that even their time with their families costs the neglect of some aspect of their job. Under this kind of pressure, only a few feel able to take on new friendships, and many of them might consider clergy as the last sort of new friend they would want. Moreover, since men in higher management have considerable power, they are constantly the target of people who want favors done for them. In fact, some are rarely approached by any who do not have a favor in mind. This tends to make them habitually insulate themselves from as many new contacts as possible; they become suspicious of anyone who approaches them with a purpose that is not quite clear.

Corporate management, like the union, is a closed structure. Unlike the union, however, it makes no claim to be democratic. Its decisions are made autocratically by individuals and committees, on private property and behind closed doors. The managers I knew did not welcome any suggestion that it should be otherwise. Hugh and I learned this the hard way. One of our earliest contacts with management took place in the private dining room of a large company, with a group of corporate staff convened to meet us by a friend in the company. We announced that we were eager to learn about the life and problems they faced in their work, and had the audacity to suggest that we might be invited to sit in as observers in some of their committee meetings.

"That's none of your business," came back the retort. "How would you like us to tell you how to baptize babies?"

In spite of these early difficulties we succeeded eventually in making friends in the offices of a number of plants and company headquarters.

Lester Perkins was one of those with whom we had talked enough so that he understood and believed in the goals of industrial mission. When we met for lunch one day I hoped he would agree to convene a group of his colleagues at the division headquarters at the end of the summer. He responded to my proposal with some ideas of his own.

"Those who tend to be naturally attracted to D.I.M. discussions," he said, "are the nonconformists, the mavericks, and maybe even the malcontents. I'm one of these myself, and as a group we tend to be different. But this isn't enough. You're bound to get a distorted view of what industrial managers are like. You need a smattering of more typical specimens. Moreover, it doesn't further D.I.M.'s prospects of winning acceptance if it gets to be the general idea that you gather around you only discontented men."

"What should I do?" I asked.

"Go to the top," he suggested. "Industrial mission takes a while to understand, and if managers feel their bosses support it, they will at least be positively disposed toward it until they feel they understand it themselves."

Hugh and I had made our way into industry at different points, and having served our apprenticeship listening and learning from individuals who had befriended us, we were beginning to try to establish discussion groups with managers. We took Lester's advice and went to the top, or at least as near the top as seemed necessary. But we found that even a manager of division staff function could be highly inaccessible. One man spoke with great cordiality on the phone but suggested that I call him in a month's time, when he expected a particular crisis would be over. Then, he felt sure, he would have time to sit down and discuss my project with me. This suggestion implied, I felt, that he did not want to brush me off. When I called the following month, however, he was away on business. Then he was in conference, and then when he called me I was out. After this he was away on vacation, until finally, three months and ten phone calls later, we met with his education and training director. When the manager at last expressed interest in industrial mission and suggested that the education and training director try to convene a group of eight personnel managers for a series of lunchtime discussions with me, I felt my persistence was paying off. But then he remarked that, in view of the coming model changeover, we had better try not to begin until October, and I knew my days of frustrated waiting were not yet done. Painful though I found it, this waiting seemed preferable to being so busy with tangential tasks that I would be otherwise occupied when an opportunity in industry opened up. Of course, while waiting for openings in one area I was sometimes absorbed in developments elsewhere. And in this period I was able to read so widely in industrial history, labor relations, and social psychology that I later found myself better read in their own field than some of the managers I knew.

THE PERSONNEL MANAGERS GROUP

When the first meeting of the group finally began, I found myself at a round table in a management dining room with eight personnel managers. Most of them were in their thirties or early forties and dealt directly or indirectly with the union. They gave me the impression of having clear eyes, strong jaws, and a decisive and forceful way of speaking. One was a Yale graduate, two others were former FBI agents, another was a one-time college football star. My description of the industrial mission and my confession that I was also meeting with union officials so intrigued them, apparently, that they agreed to my proposal for a series of lunchtime discussions on ethics and industrial relations.

This began a relationship lasting for over three years. During this period we met as a group about fifteen times, usually in the winter and spring, at monthly intervals. Immediately after eating we gathered in a conference room for an hour's discussion, launched with the presentation of a thesis by myself or some member of the group, or with a case study one of the managers and I had devised. Between meetings I sometimes lunched with the men individually, and these contacts led to several fascinating visits to the plants, during some of which I was an observer at grievance or safety committee meetings. Naturally—perhaps inevitably—much of the discussion in these meetings of the personnel managers focused on the role of the union.

Because I wanted to be provocative, but also to keep the group from combining against me and my opinions, I kicked off the first series of discussions not by asserting my own opinions but by restating some of the theses in Peter Drucker's book *The New Society.* Drucker's reputation as a distinguished industrial consultant, known to most of the group, guaranteed that his stimulating analysis of industrial society would at least be listened to. Moreover, they could attack these ideas, and either I or another member of the group could defend them, without the exchange becoming too personal. In one of the first meetings I set forth the following four points:

1. Management must be concerned primarily with profit and productivity and cannot rule primarily in the interests of its employees.

2. Only with unions standing as a power within the enterprise and taking over some of the traditional prerogatives of management can management's rule of the enterprise be legitimized.

3. Because the union must always be in opposition, its position is always insecure. It expresses this insecurity by demanding allegiance to itself against the company in order to organize the militant loyalty of its members.

4. Good industrial relations would be furthered if management tried to increase the union's sense of security and fostered a sense

among the men of "twin allegiance" instead of "split allegiance" to the company and the union.

As I stated these four propositions, a few of the managers began to mutter and groan. One of them grumbled at one point that it sounded like these statements had been written by Nikita Khrushchev. When I finished there was a vigorous expression of disagreement. The group was horrified at Drucker's suggestion that management could not rule in the employee's interests. Two managers, John and Tod, led the attack. They said their company had learned how to deal responsibly and honestly with its employees, and the union was no longer necessary. In fact, they claimed, the union was forced to make big issues out of trifles. They had not the slightest doubt that they were virtuous enough to treat their employees with complete fairness. They agreed with Drucker that the union felt insecure, but insisted that this sprang from its own redundancy.

One man enlivened the discussion by arguing strongly in defense of Drucker's position. After the meeting he approached me a little sheepishly and said, "Lest my job be in jeopardy sometime, I hope you realize my statements were made purely for the sake of argument." In subsequent discussions, he and the other members of the group gave every indication of being honestly convinced that the company had learned to deal fairly with its employees, that the unions' hate-the-company philosophy was the most damaging factor in labor-management relations, and that unions were no longer necessary and might someday even wither away.

Equally interesting to me were the group's views on industrial workers. At a later meeting I provoked a discussion on this subject by again making some points from Drucker's book:

1. Most human beings need status and function in their work, that is, they need to work at something they feel is important and have other people respect them for it.

2. Production-line work offers far too little status and function.

In making this point I mentioned that Drucker was supported by Christian writers such as Reinhold Niebuhr and Emil Brunner; social scientists such as Elton Mayo, Eli Chinoy, and Chris Argyris; and some other writers, such as Harvey Swados, who have actually worked on production lines themselves.

3. The industrial system contains nothing that inherently denies the worker status and function. But though a basic change in the system may not be necessary, if workers are to have adequate status and function concrete changes are needed in policy and practice.

I meant to go on, but the group broke in, impatiently challenging Drucker and the other authorities I had mentioned. They defended our industrial system on the grounds that it has done more than anything else in history to improve conditions, encourage workers to develop their skills, and promote men to management positions from the ranks. Most workers in industry are happy, they insisted, and those who are not are often the type who would be unhappy anywhere. If a man doesn't like it, he can get a job somewhere else. The social scientist, they suggested, knew industry only superficially.

"Of course, if you interview people and ask them if they're happy, they're going to deny it. The social psychologists from the outside don't really know the men." One of the group wrote off Harvey Swados and others who had written of their experience on the line with the comment, "Anyone who's intelligent enough to write a book is too intelligent to be happy on a production line."

"In all fairness," one of the managers admitted, "it's sometimes hard for us to appreciate that most men are happy in their work, for we give almost all our attention to a very small minority who are troublemakers and unhappy." He then described the kind of worker he believed made up the vast majority of his employees.

"He comes to work every day on time and goes right to his station on the line. When the bell rings he starts work. When the bell rings again he stops for coffee break. When the bell rings again he starts immediately. He works steadily and efficiently and never causes trouble. If he has a problem he doesn't go first to the union steward, but to his foreman. When the final bell rings he goes directly home." He smiles as he concluded his description, "And lots of these employees have pride in their work. Often I've tried to persuade them to take a better job. But no, they have been on that job for years and they don't want to change."

In these first discussions the debate was vigorous, but I was not sure that any real dialogue was taking place. I was challenging the group with provocative ideas and felt I was receiving in return the kind of canned response that precluded real encounter. I was learning from these men, but doubted whether they were learning anything from me. Certain reasons for this stood out clearly. These managers were in subordinate positions and had little to do with making policy. Most of them lived in great hope of promotion. Some feared they might be passed over. To get ahead, it seemed urgent not only to be an effective manager but also to profess a "sound business philosophy." It appeared likely that the less confident a man was about his future in the company, the more anxious he would be to prove himself a thoroughly reliable company man. I also suspected that, even if I were to acquire the brilliance of a Reinhold Niebuhr in demonstrating that the workers' understanding of the role and value of unions was based on Christian premises, still most of the group would remain unmoved. Our theology and social philosophy appeared as functions mainly of our class and vocational aspirations.

OPPORTUNITY AND FRUSTRATION

While in these early sessions I began to feel we had reached a stalemate, the managers no doubt felt a little that by presenting them with Drucker's unconventional ideas I was putting them on the spot. In the third series of discussions, when they began presenting case studies for consideration, they started in turn to put me on the spot. In one case a man raised the question of

THE WORLD OF MANAGEMENT

the ethical limits he should observe in his tactical struggles with the union committee. In a certain instance, when the company was not inclined to give a concession not provided for in the union contract, the union built up a bank of minor grievances on strikable issues. When he refused to settle as the union demanded, it threatened a strike. But before the strike was called, the union subtly indicated that if the concession were granted, the grievances would be withdrawn and the strike averted.

On the other hand, by granting the concession the manager sacrificed the company's interest by setting a costly precedent. There seemed to be no way out but to fight fire with fire. The brother of the chief union steward also worked in the plant. He arrived at his work station thirty seconds late after lunch, left his work station without authorization the next day, and infringed the rules on several other occasions. He and two or three other relatives and friends of the union leadership were vulnerable to harassment if not discipline by the management, and a few well-placed hints about it could pressure the union to reconsider its strike threat.

"But once this kind of tactic is allowed," said the manager, "step by step you often find yourself led into increasingly unsavory practices." The whole group seemed to identify with this problem, and in their comments opened their hearts and pressed me for answers.

"Of course," said one of them, "we don't expect you to tie up any of these specific problems for us, but can't you give us a framework within which we can wrestle through them ourselves with some degree of ethical clarity? For instance, do you believe the end justifies the means?"

I squirmed, as all the precepts of ethical decision-making I had studied in past years raced through my mind and shattered on the hard specifics of the problem. The moment of truth had come, and the best I could offer was the suggestion that in this cold war between management and union perhaps the tactics to be used might themselves be subject to negotiation and agreement. Each side could be damaged by the unscrupulous tactics of the other. Perhaps, then, each would agree to desist so as not to be hurt itself.

My feelings were mixed when I discovered a few days later that the suggestion was neither new nor impractical. Tod had invited me to spend the afternoon with him in his plant observing him at work. His main piece of business was a session with the union committee to discuss union complaints that foremen, the supervisors who make up the lowest rank of management, were working on production jobs contrary to the union contract. I was surprised that so much of the session with the union was taken up with bantering back and forth. Even when charges were thrown heatedly at the other side, often as not the roughness was turned by a flip remark of some sort. Although there was some talk about the possibility of the company writing yet another letter to the foremen asking them not to do production work, and although Mickey, the union chairman, teased management with little homilies about doing good and life everlasting, nothing much seemed to result from the two-hour discussion. Yet Tod indicated that the meeting had given union representatives an opportunity to blow off steam and report to the membership that they had given management hell. For his own part, he had had a chance to tell union leadership once more some home truths about the pressures of competition and the necessity of reducing labor costs.

Two things particularly fascinated me. The first was the way the strength of union and management were checked against each other. Each side seemed to have the power to make life miserable for—but not to destroy—the other. The result was a certain measure of respect and moderation in demand. Thus Tod and Mickey recognized each other as pretty reasonable and decent guys. And they realized the advantage of having a reasonable and decent opposite number. They also recognized that if either took advantage of the other when he made a mistake, and drove too hard a bargain, the other might not remain reasonable and decent. And since Mickey was just as aware of the company's pressure on Tod as Tod was of the union membership's pressure on Mickey, both found it easy to avoid rocking the boat. The constant pressure from the one kept labor costs from getting too high, and the constant pressure from the other made sure that the ordinary workers were not outrageously mistreated. The result: a certain equilibrium.

My second observation was sharpened by a conversation with Tod after the committee had departed. Throughout these negotiations, it appeared, much was going on below the level of speech. The responsibilities of each party were so complex and intertwined that simple moral precepts seemed practically useless. Discussion raged over the charge that foremen were violating the contract by engaging in production work. Although the contract clearly states that foremen shall not work, apparently again and again the union found them working. If the company really wanted them to observe the contract, it could bring them in line simply by firing the first man caught working, or merely disciplining them.

But the company apparently did not really want the foremen to have their hands tied in this way. And after all it was not a big matter. The result was that Tod, as personnel manager, found himself in a position where it was impossible to be entirely honest with the union committee. To admit to the committee that the company had no intention of enforcing this clause in the contract would not only be accusing his own outfit of bad faith, but also inviting the union to violate the contract in reprisal. If he admitted to the committee that foremen were working and he could do nothing about it, the committee members would demand to meet with somebody who could, and Tod's usefulness to the company would be at an end.

The result of this situation was endless play-acting in the conference room.

"Foreman Jones was working. You've got to put an end to that."

"Who says so?"

"I do."

"Did you see him?"

"No."

"How do you know, then?"

"John Smith told me."

"Did John Smith actually see him working?"

"Yes."

"How do you know John Smith was telling the truth?" (John Smith is a union steward with considerable political power.)

"Simply because I trust John Smith."

"Maybe Smith was wrong."

"He tells me he was sure. He reported the foreman had on work gloves and worked on that press up there for half an hour."

"How do you know he wasn't mistaken? Anyone can make a mistake. As a matter of fact, I asked Jones if he was working, and he says he wasn't."

"But Smith says he was."

"Are you saying Jones is dishonest?"

"I'm saying he was working. Smith saw him, and I trust Smith."

"Well, I trust Jones." Then, with a reconciling touch of benevolence, Tod said, "OK. I'm not convinced that Jones was working, but I'll speak to him about it."

This gesture might not prove to be enough to satisfy the union, and if they found witnesses and wrote up a grievance they could press the case against foreman Jones even to arbitration. However, not only does grievance procedure take months to follow through to an arbitrator's decision, but it is very expensive, and even if the union won, the worst that could happen to the company would be that it would be forced to pay the employee who might have done the half hour of work the foreman actually did.

What was more, even though Tod might be aware that Jones had been working, how could the union committeemen be sure that Smith wasn't lying? The union knew that the company was not seriously trying to enforce this clause and that Tod was putting on an act in pretending it was, but what could the union do? And what else could Tod do?

Through discussions of this case and others, the group of personnel managers and I vividly experienced the inadequacy of the Golden Rule and other simple ethical formulas usually taught by the churches. But the group still hoped I might offer them something useful and urged me to spend a whole session in presenting them with some ways in which our religion might help them in their decision-making. I saw this as my great opportunity and seriously tried to spell out a way by which social goals and policies could be derived from theological doctrines. I suggested, for instance, that since the goods of this earth are for all men to enjoy and to share justly, a possible Christian goal for industry might be to end the distinction between salaried and hourly-rated employees and put the whole work force on salary. I knew that such a suggestion would be challenged. (This was long before any prominent industrialists and conservative economists had supported a guaranteed annual income.) But I felt the group had known me long enough and trusted me enough to discuss with me this and other "dangerous" ideas. Although somebody asked if the social goals suggested were pro-union, the group as a whole seemed more curious than hostile in their comments. Unfortunately, another group scheduled to use the conference room forced us to suspend our discussion prematurely. Nevertheless, I had a sense of elation driving home that day because I felt at last we were nearing pay dirt.

A few days later—"I feel as if someone has been trying to sabotage our group," said Ken, the training director, on the phone. My elation faded as he continued, "My boss, Pat Gromer, is upset. Somebody told him you planned to discuss in the group the forbidden subject of union bargaining goals. Pat had most of the men in the group canvassed and found they couldn't see where the discussions were getting. So he decided the meetings weren't doing the company any good, they apparently weren't helping you, and they should stop. I don't know who talked to Pat—I can't imagine anyone telling him these things. Of course, in our last meeting we didn't have time to get everything thrashed out, but I didn't think anyone was upset. And if they were, why didn't they come to me?"

I wondered why Pat had not seen fit to talk to me and asked Ken if I should see him.

"No, you'd better not, at least not now. He's too upset."

Apparently as soon as an unidentified employee registered an ambiguous complaint to an inaccessible manager, the latter had decided that my work there had to stop. There was nothing I could do, at least for the time being.

Perhaps I shall never altogether understand what was really the problem. I knew only that for the first time I had assumed the role of lecturer to them, and thus shattered the image of myself as a "safe" listener, one who could do unpaid public relations work for the company. I had become a teacher, a suspiciously radical teacher, of things they could neither predict nor control. I could appreciate that the thought of proliferating unpredictable and uncontrollable elements in the organization might give any administrator nightmares. On the other hand, the fear of such free discussion as I had known in British industry had never expressed itself so clearly. Ironically, it seemed that freedom of speech was more limited in the institutions of American "free enterprise" than in the corporate structures of "socialist" Britain. One found oneself wondering if this habit of submitting docilely to control of discussion in industry might increasingly spill over into American political life.

I never had an opportunity to share these questions with Pat, but a few weeks later Hugh did talk the situation over with both Ken, the training director, and Pat, his boss. Ken indicated that several things seemed to be bothering Pat and he seemed almost eager to find some reason to end the meetings. Two weeks earlier I had arranged a tour for some clergymen through one of his plants, and in the course of it a plant manager had been asked some sort of embarrassing question by one of the visitors. Although I was not present, Pat somehow held me responsible. Ken had also heard Pat complain about my testifying before the State Affairs Committee on civil rights legislation in Lansing and about my "socialistic background" from England. But when Hugh talked to him personally he would not discuss any of these things. All he would say was that my approach was too theoretical—impractical—and that the men themselves did not see how the meetings could be of any use.

"Of course I have nothing but respect for Scott," he said. But he made clear that he would consider a proposal from Hugh for reconvening the meetings in six months, if I were not involved.

This experience upset me as much as anything else that happened in Detroit. It made me wonder not only whether I was suited for the work, but also whether management would ever allow the kind of freedom necessary if significant dialogue were to take place.

FIVE

❦❦❦❦❦

The Gospel of Work

IN SPITE OF the setback with the Personnel Managers Group, my contacts with other managers continued to multiply, and through repeated visits and lunches and long conversations a variety of relationships began to grow up. I found the openness with which they talked astonishing, and the picture of the world they described gripping, fascinating, and sometimes savage. For many it seemed that work was their life, and they lusted for it and for its rewards with a passion. In return, the work often demanded that they be completely dedicated and utterly single-minded toward their jobs. Every effort must be made to succeed, and the competition required that every aspect of a man's life be totally directed toward this end. One production-control manager explained that, like many of his colleagues, he arrives at work at 7:15 in the morning after a thirty-five-minute drive from home and often stays until after six at night. Even then he frequently takes a briefcase full of papers home with him. When I asked if he felt overworked, he seemed surprised by the ques-

74

tion and replied, "When the plant's running, during the day, I don't have time to think, but if I can have an hour alone before things start in the morning and another after they quiet down at night, I can do the hard creative thinking my job needs."

Most managers seemed to feel that the demands of their jobs were not exorbitant. Effective job performance promised the great prize of regular promotion, and the job itself often proved both absorbing and satisfying. On one occasion an assembly plant manager and his personnel department head described in some detail their operations, goals, and point of view. What stood out was the pride and contagious enthusiasm they had for their work. Their greatest satisfaction, they said, was to see the quality line on the graph steadily rising and the cost line steadily going down. Their total absorption in the problems of production and their success in solving them gave them a solid, satisfying sense that they were achieving something. They seemed to find the main meaning of life in their work.

The inverse also appeared to be true. Separation from their work was a kind of psychological death. To be forcibly separated was to be "murdered," to lose the sense of identity—to become, in the words of George Orwell, "an unperson." One former executive of a big corporation who had a high position overseas returned for the sake of his family to the United States. Finding no job available in his own company here, he joined the management of a smaller outfit, where he worked for almost five years. Then a reorganization program within top management ended with his being laid off without notice. He said his life in the past six months had been one of frustration, humiliation, and despair. He beat every bush in sight and everywhere the answer was the same: "We're sorry. You're fifty years old and we wouldn't think of taking you on at your age." He even applied for a factory job as a laborer, but was told, "We can't use you, you're too old." As he finished the story he fled from the room and burst into tears in the bathroom.

His wife said she did not dare leave him alone.

Sometimes the psychological "murders" are committed with spine-chilling premeditation. A friend who worked in a very large corporation told me how his company had got rid of a vice-president the year before. Since he was unpopular and had not proved a success, it was decided he must go. However, not only was he a difficult man to handle, but only if he resigned would the company be free of responsibility to him. Accordingly, at a secret meeting of all the vice-presidents except himself and one who was his ally, a company psychologist was brought in to advise them how to carry on the kind of psychological harassment that would cause him to resign. I did not hear the details of the campaign except that when he gave an order to be mimeographed, the typing pool would send it back typed to read in the opposite sense from his instructions. He resigned on a Wednesday soon after, and was off company premises by Friday.

For many the threat of losing one's job is not as great as the possibility of being consigned to a position in the corporate backwater remote from the channels of promotion. For instance, a forty-five-year-old manager described his expert skill in a specialized area of the company organization. In this specialty he had advanced about as far as possible within the company. He had likewise developed the potential of his particular kind of work to the utmost of his capacity. Since he had grown accustomed to a high salary, it was hard for him to contemplate resigning and enduring the comparative poverty of a new and congenial job. He finds himself, therefore, facing the grim prospect of spending the next twenty years in a job he has already mastered, which can offer him very few new challenges or opportunities for growth.

"The lives of my associates are also marked by fear," he observed as we sat in the executive dining room. "It's not that we're not well paid or afraid of unfair dismissal, but we're afraid of losing what we have, or not achieving what we hope, or somehow just not 'making it.'"

Of course such fear is not universal. Perhaps for most it functions as a gnawing anxiety which waxes and wanes just below the level of consciousness. This causes managers to invest their superiors with informal powers of great magnitude. I felt in them on occasions an almost doglike eagerness to please the boss, to anticipate his desires and so win his approval. A plant manager told me that if he started smoking a pipe, within a few days perhaps half his department heads would be smoking pipes as well. A few years earlier he had begun taking courses at night school. The power of his example was such that now his staff includes a higher percentage of managers studying at night than any other of the company's plants.

This almost pathetic eagerness to win approval inhibited a manager I had known since college days from introducing me to his superior, who he suspected might not approve of me. On the other hand, I remember on at least one occasion a man who had little interest in the industrial mission expressing great cordiality because he thought it might please his boss.

The Plant Management Group

At the end of the service in a suburban church at which I had preached one summer Sunday morning, a man who introduced himself as Harold Bayne expressed interest in the industrial mission and proposed that we lunch in town sometime the next week. When we got together I discovered that he was manager of a nearby manufacturing plant of a large corporation. He questioned me closely about my work and eventually said he wanted me to meet his personnel manager and discuss the possibilities of forming a group of his management team. He declined to take part himself, on the grounds that since he was the plant manager his presence would inhibit discussion. Two lunches and three conversations later, the plant personnel manager Jim Hoffman and I had become friends and had found seven departmental managers

78 DETROIT INDUSTRIAL MISSION

willing to participate. In addition to Jim, these included the production manager, the plant engineer, and the production control
and quality control managers. All the men held positions at a comparable level in the plant hierarchy and were between thirty-five
and forty-five years old. It was not a highly sophisticated group,
but what they lacked in polish they made up for in aggressiveness
and passionate devotion to their job. Though none was an Ivy
League graduate and few read very much, most of them continued
to take professional and business courses at night school, and all
were active churchmen.

Whereas the earlier group of personnel managers had begun by
discussing questions relating to industrial structure and corporate
policy, this one began with case studies which centered on questions of individual ethics. For instance, one of our first meetings
dealt with the need to fire an employee. The question posed was
how to square the unavoidable cruelty involved with the Christian
command to be kind. In this session they argued, perhaps predictably, that it was a disservice to a man who was not performing
his job to maintain him in continued employment on work for
which he was not suited. In the long run, they reasoned, the
kindest course was to let him go, so that he could find work in
which he could excel and be happy.

We had met four or five times when the plant manager retired,
and a member of the group, Stu Sinclair, was promoted to his
position. Though he had become their superior, he remained a
part of the group and considered himself still "one of the boys."
The meetings continued, at first seemingly unaffected by his new
status.

With this group one of the most significant case studies was
about a supervisor who turned down a promotion rather than
sacrifice his work on the city council and the quality of his family
life. My point of view in this instance was that no institution has
the right to claim a man's whole life or absolute loyalty, and the
supervisor should therefore not suffer the disapproval of his fellow

managers for his decision. By the end of our talk some of the managers saw this, but the idea made them highly uncomfortable. In the course of discussion they tried by every possible means to work it so that the supervisor could keep his extracurricular activities and still accept the promotion. One remarked that a man with "real stuff" could do all these things. Another assumed that by refusing to accept the promotion he would "stop growing" and to that degree waste his life.

"The corporation wants a blank check on your time and energy," it was explained to me. "They want the very best of your life. They want you to give yourself to them and not hold anything back." The words "In Him do all things cohere," went through my mind as I remembered sermons I had heard about Christ as the center and proper unifying force in life. According to this idea our loyalties to country, family, and even church should be at most partial and critical. We owe them service only to the degree that they serve the cause of Chirst. But for these men this did not seem to be an option. They were telling me that their lives were already organized around another well-established center.

"And we want to give ourselves absolutely," my friend continued, "because that's the price of success. And if you're like me, you want to succeed more than anything." When I reiterated my thought that no one should give himself absolutely to any institution, he exclaimed, "What you're saying is against human nature!"

I was not sure it was against human nature, but it was certainly against the culture of these industrial managers. Another time Jim Hoffman complained, "I can't understand why some men would rather be laid off for a while than work." The two men he told me about were blue-collar workers and did not seem to need the money desperately, since their wives worked; so they valued the opportunity to loaf for a couple of weeks more than the additional cash. It struck me that these two men had a view perhaps common to preindustrial society, i.e.: "Work until you have enough to satisfy immediate needs and then relax." This is still conspicuously the rule in some parts of the underdeveloped world. Whereas in our modern thinking about work we have a curious contradiction. On the one hand, we regard it as valuable only for the money it supplies; that is, it does not carry a moral commitment. On the other, we think of the man who does not want to work as being somehow immoral. It is almost as if we regarded it a sin to be content with little and a virtue to be consumed with avarice in the form of an obsession about "getting ahead."

It is small wonder that Jim could not understand these work-shy employees in his plant, for his philosophy of work and theirs represent views as far as possible from each other. Jim told me that he was studying law at night school and might leave the company in due course because he felt his opportunities for advancement were slim. His dynamic conception of himself and his job assumed that as one grows older one's abilities should grow. Thus unless one is regularly promoted to bigger and more responsible jobs, one becomes automatically a misfit and a failure.

Such an outlook can drive men to great achievement, but it also molds their personalities and sometimes makes them like souls possessed. In one week, for instance, I lunched with two men who had recently become managers of their respective plants. One had been plant manager for only a few weeks. Perhaps my asking him how it felt made him nervous, but he talked almost constantly, speaking with the confident manner of one who has things pretty well figured out. He banged his fist lightly on the lunch table and seemed to be trying to win assent to his position by his many words and the force of his personality. He recounted how he had become a success—and how on the day of the announcement of his appointment as plant manager he stayed in the plant until he had shaken the hand of every supervisor and department head, to thank them for the cooperation which had made his promotion possible. Then he went to his wife to tell her the good news and how he had thanked "all the supervisors and assistants except one."

"Who's that?" she asked. And then he thanked her, and she

cried. He told how he handled his wife, by the same principles of labor relations as he used at the plant.

The other manager spoke informally at lunch to a group of ministers I had arranged to have visit his plant. He had been under terrific pressure during the model changeover, and he showed it by his nervous, tense, preoccupied manner. He talked freely, even compulsively, in answer to the ministers' questions. He had held five jobs with the company, for none of which he had been qualified, but which, by dint of showing proper aggressiveness and enthusiasm, he performed successfully. Two or three times he changed jobs because he realized that the work he was doing would be for him a dead end. He was determined to get ahead.

This man rises each day at 5:45 A.M., talks to his wife at breakfast, and arrives at work at 7:30. The day is for him a series of meetings and conferences and interviews where he has to make decisions and infect his team with enthusiasm. One of his biggest problems is to keep his team in good communication with each other and win high, quality production from the workers. He usually leaves for home at 6:30, and after supper reads the plant mail he has brought from the office.

Here was a man whose responsibilities so possessed him that whenever he was not actually talking or being directly addressed, it was as if a veil fell across his eyes, and in his mind he seemed to be wrestling with a production problem. I am sure he was conscious that, unless he produced, he would not long be the plant manager. But he also seemed to enjoy his work immensely. It absorbed, excited, and challenged him. For all its problems, it offered him colossal satisfactions. Their price was to have the job almost consume him.

Such overwhelming pressure was experienced by many managers I knew. Sometimes, I gathered, miscalculations, poor management, or unavoidable mishaps built up the force of it. Moreover, top management apparently delays many major decisions as long as possible, so as to make them in the light of the last report on the moves of competition. This means that once decisions are made, nothing less than a crash program suffices to implement them in time. I was told that a better car could be produced if model changes were made less frequently, but that the dealers press for a semiannual change because the public always wants something new. (One wonders a little if the public naturally and inevitably wants something new, or has been led to crave novelty by years of exposure to advertising. The next logical step would be a model change every three months.)

In our industrial system the sense of a metaphysical absolute has vanished, giving way to the imperative of infinite acceleration. Everything must move faster, grow bigger, become more profitable. There is no limit. The notions of a just price, fair profits, and adequate growth have been replaced by the rule of the maximum. Our goals are thought of as selling as dear as possible—buying as cheaply as possible—so as to make as much profit as possible—so as to raise the standard of living as high as possible. This is usually defended on the grounds that it furnishes a dynamic which drives our economy to ever more spectacular achievements. However, it might be attacked on the ground that it falsifies the real situation and subordinates human needs to the dynamics of the system. To say that we must seek maximum profits, even in the long run, implies that other values and goals that do not serve this aim should be sacrificed. A goal of maximum profit, or indeed maximum anything, tends to subject us to tremendous pressures which drive, drive, and drive us.

At one meeting I read to the Plant Management Group a paper I had written on productivity. Their comments were critical. Although some allowed it was well written, they felt it was negative, overpessimistic, and unappreciative of the good of industrial achievements. I defended it on the grounds that, since we had agreed as to the value of increasing productivity, little would be gained by merely reaffirming this in the paper.

To my surprise the plant engineer responded, "But we need to be reassured that increased productivity is a worthy goal and thoroughly good objective—" It occurred to me that he was crying out for reassurance because of his sensitivity to the human price exacted by our achievements.

This discussion led to the suggestion that I report to the group what I had learned from them about the application of Christianity to industry. I did so with some anxiety, for fear it might lead to a disaster similar to my experience with the Personnel Managers Group. I spoke, therefore, rather less ambitiously, simply describing what I had observed as a result of my theological concerns. I began gently, commenting on the moral ambiguity of decisions made in industry and the responsible way in which they generally seemed to be made. Then I raised certain questions as to the meaning or purpose of these men's lives as revealed in our earlier discussions. First I observed that the managers in the group did not seem to sense that their work was part of their service to God. Although corporations sometimes won from them an almost idolatrous devotion, they ascribed to it little if any high sense of purpose. And they personally were given to no great cause beyond themselves. I said this on the basis of life goals as they had described them to me. One man, for example, wanted simply to "get ahead," to be successful. Another hoped to save $100,000 by the time he was fifty-five, so that he could retire and move to Florida, sell a little insurance, and relax.

I continued with the point that, so far as these men had shown, to them God seemed entirely absent from industry. He had no purposes and was not active there. Even in the area of moral choice, it was not religious sanctions but "good business practice" that justified their decisions. I hazarded the possibility that for them the American industrial system played the role of God in the world. They certainly showed that they did not question it. For them the system was the Given, and they tended to judge other men on the basis of how well they served the system rather than judging the system in terms of how well it served human beings.

No debate or disagreement followed these comments or broke into them; instead the group said they felt my observations were perceptive and true. But the issue seemed not to concern them. Though all the men were more or less dedicated churchmen, their private admissions to me before and after the discussion did nothing but further support my thesis.

"I believe in the deity," began Bill Ostrowski. Throughout his adult life he had attended a Protestant church because it "made him feel good," and sent his children to Sunday school so that they would learn good morals. He said he liked the minister and enjoyed his sermons, but could think of no instance in which they related significantly to his work. He agreed with me that faith ought to relate to work, but was unable to think how it could. He was only sure that in times of sickness and trouble it was nice to have the church there.

Jim Hoffman, formerly a Congregationalist, was at this time preparing for confirmation in the Episcopal Church. He declared that the change of church did not require any change in his theology. At the same time he agreed with me that God seemed entirely absent from the life of industry, and that if God was not everywhere He was not anywhere. I still could not escape a sense of surprise and dismay when I realized that for him it really did not matter whether God was present in the world of industry or not. But he stopped short of stating the syllogism's conclusion: that for him God's presence anywhere was a matter of indifference. I felt like the priest in Albert Camus' book *The Stranger*, who visits the hero in his death cell. When he presents to the condemned man the possibility of God's existence and love, the stranger responds that he is not interested in God, and with so little time left to live he cannot waste it on matters that do not interest him.

At lunch with a group of ministers I brought in to tour his plant, Stu Sinclair affirmed flatly that he never consciously made a business decision on the basis of his understanding of Christianity. His decisions, he said, were made on the basis of right and wrong, right being good business practice and wrong being whatever is detrimental to business. This forthright statement was a shock to the clergy, to the point of being puzzling, almost mysterious to them. I overheard two of them discussing it afterward.

"He couldn't have meant it was never any use," one was saying. "Even if his religion didn't consciously guide him, unconsciously it must have helped him." (I don't suppose even Stu could be certain that religion had not helped him unconsciously.)

So far apart were the two worlds that the irony was missed by both sides. Stu could not conceive of how religious faith could be relevant to his work, while the clergy literally could not believe that it was not. The manager looked on the ministers with incomprehension and indifference; they looked on him with disbelief. Neither side could manage to confront honestly the practical atheism in the situation, and by implication in our industrial society.

If any member of the group could see the significance of religious faith for industrial work, it should have been Ron Harkins. He was both a department manager and a Mormon minister, with an alert mind and some theological training. I hoped that perhaps in his own person the dialogue between church and industry might be carried on with particular acumen. First I asked him a general question as to whether he thought it possible for managers to see their work as part of their service to God.

He answered, "Perhaps it's possible, but it's highly unlikely. They don't have time to think in those terms."

"What about yourself?" I went on. "Don't you think about it?"

"Yes, but I can think more about the religious significance of my work when I get home. And then the most I can do is ask myself sometimes about the justice of things I've done. Besides, to think about work as service to God is inappropriate, somehow—it isn't helpful. It doesn't really mean anything." So in this case the double role of minister-manager did not integrate the religious and industrial styles of life, but rather divided the man and forced him to live a different life in each sphere.

DEATH OF A DIALOGUE

This impasse led me to invite Hugh to join me for support when Stu Sinclair and Jim Hoffman agreed to discuss the future of the group over lunch a few months later. Since the turmoil of the summer model changeover was past, I had hopes that we might reconvene the group for another series of discussions. I was uneasy, however, because at our last conversation they had resisted various suggestions regarding possible subjects for the next discussion series, and neither had been possible to reach by phone all summer. At the beginning of lunch I thought it a little ominous that Jim did not mention receiving phone messages from me, and both men seemed a trifle nervous. However, we soon became absorbed in talk about a pressing plant problem, which might have consumed the whole lunch hour had we not called a halt and raised the question of D.I.M. discussions at the plant. Stu responded that he felt the group could go no further in the present vein without becoming repetitious, and any other approach he feared would become downright religious.

"And religion just isn't our field," he protested. "We feel unnatural and completely beyond our depth when it's discussed. Even in my own church I avoid it and stick to counting money and serving on the properties committee."

"Have the discussions been too religious up till now?" I asked.

"No, but we're afraid they'll get that way," he answered.

Nevertheless, after some further conversation they agreed to another series of group meetings if we promised not to become overtly religious and to concentrate our attention on current work issues. This promise we readily made.

The series took place as planned, and as I sensed our work at that location was in trouble, Hugh's participation in the meetings gave me great support. Jim Hoffman led off with a typical discussion on the subject of "the best way of inspiring men with enthusiasm for their job." He contended that it was merely necessary for the manager to be alert, aggressive, and enthusiastic himself, and then his subordinates would follow his example. Without explicitily disagreeing, the rest of the group added other suggestions for promoting optimum work performance. These included judicious use of salary increases, an annual performance review, and (as Stu kept emphasizing) the big stick of fear. But all in all, no one was very daring in his suggestions, and the discussion never really got off the ground. Nobody in the group admitted that motivation was a serious problem. Although it did not peter out, this discussion of enthusiasm definitely lacked that quality.

Something interesting had happened to the group. Clearly it was dying. My guess as to the reason was confirmed by a department manager when we lunched alone together the week before its last meeting. Since taking charge of the plant a year earlier, Stu Sinclair had faced some critical management problems which not only put him under great pressure but also led him to crack the whip over the managers in the group. At first he succeeded in remaining "one of the boys," but more and more the subordinate managers began to defer to him. They hesitated to disagree with him in a group meeting, and if Stu expressed disagreement with a position already taken, the manager involved either shifted his ground— explaining that when you come right down to it he really did agree with Stu—or withdrew from the discussion and let his silence imply assent. This change came about so gradually that Stu probably did not realize it had taken place. And unfortunately, neither the managers in the group nor I felt he was secure enough, or felt secure enough ourselves, to tell him our view of the situation.

In these circumstances fruitful discussion was impossible, and the series ended with the next meeting. The subject was "The Labor Movement Today," and the debate was far more open and lively than at the two or three previous meetings. But when, at the end of the hour, I observed that the group could not discuss current problems very freely in that context and that our series should therefore terminate, Stu immediately agreed. With a sense of relief we said "goodby" and with smiles and friendliness promised to keep in touch.

POST-MORTEM AND NEW BEGINNINGS

Although I shared the sense of relief, I had once more a feeling of defeat and bafflement. The end of this dialogue and the earlier forced dissolution of the Personnel Managers Group were two eminent failures in my work in Detroit. Certainly I had succeeded in the first task of mission mentioned in Chapter One, for I had established contact with men on the scene of their industrial involvement. But in tasks 2 and 3, to evolve new theological understanding and create groups with their own momentum, we failed. And because of this, it seemed, our success in the first task could be only temporary.

Several factors combined to produce the failure. The pressure for autocratic control in the organization of the corporation itself obviously played a part. With the personnel managers I think I won the trust of the men in the group. But since their superior did not attend the meetings, he did not share the same degree of trust, and his anxieties forced him to end our meetings. In the case of the plant management group, on the other hand, the plant manager himself participated in the group and his anxieties could be dealt with directly. But his presence so inhibited his subordinates that honest discussion died. A more subtle form of lack of freedom lay in the self-discipline generated in the industrial work place itself. This concentrates attention on practical and

THE WORLD OF MANAGEMENT

immediate tasks. An engineer in the Plant Managers Group told me early in our contact that, to keep interested, he would need a specific goal and a certain assurance that he would learn something of value to his work.

"We could talk about that all day and not get anywhere," said another engineer when I raised the issue of President Kennedy's crackdown on the steel industry. "Let's get back to work."

In the culture of the Middle Ages, scientific and technical curiosity was discouraged lest men's minds be drawn away from the theological issues essential to their salvation. By a strange reversal and through comparable discipline, men in modern industry perhaps resist the impulse to speculate about larger issues, lest their minds be drawn away from the immediate concerns of their ambition and their livelihood.

In both management groups, however, we came to the threshold of serious grappling with the ethical and religious dimensions of industrial work. With the personnel managers the sense of moral conflict experienced in dealing with the union focused the issue. When at the end I insisted that the particular moral dilemmas they posed could only be dealt with by considering the justice of our industrial system, I was ruled out of order. In the Plant Management Group the question was posed in terms of the personal price the men themselves paid in their furious concentration on their work. They knew that through their concentration they won personal rewards and contributed to our dynamic economy. They also knew that they were paying a considerable human price. I felt that an awareness of this price was what led some of them to look to me and to the industrial mission with hope. Perhaps we could provide them with a vision that would make them believe the human price they were paying was well spent. Because of my own doubts I could not reassure them, and they were disappointed.

Our discussions may have foundered as we neared the religious conflict they dimly perceived, which I did not honestly face. Their commitment may indeed have been to their company and beyond that to the industrial system. They may have sensed that my commitment lay elsewhere. In any case they found it consistently difficult to agree with me when I urged that their jobs and the system deserved at most only partial and critical loyalty.

My disappointment retreated before the sense that to have come this far with these groups was no mean achievement. Moreover, to have moved so far that these men could admit their hunger for answers which clearly have theological and Christian dimensions further convinced me that my job was worth doing.

Other members of the D.I.M. staff had been engaged in parallel discussions in other industrial locations, and soon I became involved in two new groups meeting successively in a big corporate headquarters. These series were convened over a period of two years by the company's education and training department, which also sponsored discussion series on great books. The department drew men from most of the big corporate offices, but recruited them without the subtle psychological pressure to participate that must have been present in the two groups just described. Hence they represented a more varied and voluntary constituency.

Here I began with case studies bearing on the personal crises men face at work. Only at the end of the series did we begin to touch on questions of social and industrial policy. From beginning to end, these series were stimulating, fun, and well attended. They neither died nor were forcibly stopped; each ended after six meetings, according to our initial plan. In these two series we began again to build the kind of trust that would make honesty possible and the kind of personal friendships that assured me regular contact at the headquarters whether or not a discussion series was in progress. This experience gave me both immense pleasure and the hope that here we might also more successfully press forward in the task of theological discovery. But because of my departure from Detroit I had to leave this hope in the hands of my colleagues on the D.I.M. staff.

Unexpectedly, before I left, from the area of my second defeat a heart-warming incident came to reassure me. I had not seen Ron Harkins since we said goodby at the last meeting of the Plant Management Group two years before. I knew he had moved to a position at company headquarters, so was not surprised to meet him there in one of the corridors. The warmth of his greeting did surprise me, as did the immediacy with which he began to share with me the complexities of a hard decision he was then facing.

"I've just come from a meeting with the management of the Manufacturing Division. Two months ago I refused their offer to become a manager in the assembly plant in Ohio. That offer came only two weeks after I had accepted the chairmanship of the school committee. I'm not sure they appreciated my reluctance to move, and I know they'll resent it if I refuse the offer they're making now. The new plant on the other side of town is in a terrible mess. The whole thing seems to have been badly planned, and one problem after another has kept production and quality down and raised costs outrageously high. And the morale is shot to pieces. The division management hopes that with my help on production planning and control the new manager there can make a go of it. They feel they need me in that spot so desperately, it's an embarrassment to them that they can't stick to their original offer of a solid promotion. The most they can do is give me a salary that's tops in my classification—an increase over what I get now and the most I could get while holding my present job. They can also offer me the possibility of becoming plant manager over there if I make a go of it, when the present manager moves on. Of course it's such a challenge, I might fail, and then I'd be washed up. But they've gone so far out on a limb to get me there, I don't see how they could afford to let me fail.

"This offer was made very kindly," he went on. "A transcript of the conversation wouldn't show anything. But by tone of voice, innuendo, and facial expression they've made it quite clear that if I refuse, they feel my potential usefulness to the division is at an end. This is the last offer I'll ever receive from them. And if I stay where I am, my boss on his retirement will probably be replaced by one of these same managers whose ill will I would have earned by refusing. In other words they made it very plain, not only that the job they were offering was attractive, but that it might not be altogether healthy for me to refuse."

Ron paused.

"I want to emphasize that they were awfully nice about it all," he repeated. "But though it's an attractive offer, I still have reservations. In spite of the fact that my immediate supervisor is hard to get along with, I like the job I have now. I like to travel. There's a good chance of advancement here. Besides, the new plant is such a long way from home that if I take the job there I'll have to resign from the school committee and almost give up seeing my family, unless we move. But a move right now wouldn't be good for the family."

Together, Ron and I explored the factors involved in this decision at considerable length until he departed for his office, where he planned to list the pro's and con's in parallel columns. He had to submit his decision by 8:30 the following morning.

I went home pondering his dilemma. In spite of its drawbacks, I began to feel that maybe he should take the new job. After all, he was needed there. It was where he could be most useful—there was the real opportunity and challenge. But since this was only my silent opinion, of whose soundness I was not altogether certain, it was with curiosity that I called the next day and asked, "Ron, how did you decide?"

"I refused the job," he answered. "I told them that from their point of view my reasons would probably seem entirely unreasonable, but that for personal reasons I would not accept their kind offer."

My surprise was compounded when he gave me his simple explanation.

"I couldn't accept a job when it was offered along with a threat, however veiled. I felt it showed a certain contempt for me that

I couldn't live with. It was the wrong footing to start out on. Most likely I'm *persona non grata* now in the Manufacturing Division. But this is a big company. The man I talked to told me, 'Bixby (my boss) must have gotten to you.'

" 'No,' I said, 'I take full responsibility for this decision myself. Nobody got to me.' And I feel sure I'm right, Scott," he added. "I shan't regret it."

Somehow, surprised as I was, I too felt that his decision was the right one, for by it he had broken loose from the fetters of threats and promises and made a declaration of his freedom as a Christian man. That men can and should do this was my main affirmation in our discussion series two years earlier. I had thought that the offer presented him with a life-and-death choice. And indeed, it had been so, and he chose life.

"It was providential that we met in the corridor yesterday," he said just before he hung up. I hoped he meant by this that God's grace had used me as a means to help him reach his decision. That meeting also gave me a glimpse of the glory of God.

III
THE STRUGGLE
WITH THE CHURCHES

❦ ❦ ❦

SIX

♥♥♥♥♥♥

THE PARISH ASSOCIATION

IT IS EVER THE temptation of religion to put God in a box, exclude Him from the important areas of our lives, and try to consign Him to a specific locale where He can be controlled and His influence restricted. "COMES OUT ONLY ON REQUEST" is the label we like to put on the box.

Church buildings stand as boxes built for God. Here is the holy place, here God is present. Here we can find Him when we want Him. The next step is to engage full-time ministers who will represent God to us. We expect of them the high moral standards we no longer expect of ourselves. We assign them a religious sphere of operations which we can enter when we want to, but which will not encroach upon the rest of our activities. This idea that the sphere of God's activity can be confined to a specifically religious area in our lives, and to the institution of the church, breeds at least a part of the embarrassment and hostility met by missioners in industry.

A suburban pastor told me of walking to his church one week-

end along a path that was open to his neighbors' backyards. A
great many of them were in their gardens raking, digging, swim-
ming, and drinking beer. When they saw him they tried to hide
the beer and tittered and waved and looked sheepish. Another
pastor had the inverse experience of feeling embarrassed and trying
to obscure himself behind his car when he was washing it one
Sunday afternoon, as the pious walked by on their way to visit the
church. A powerful conspiracy seeks to keep both God and the
clergy fulfilling the safe and unctuous roles expected of them.

When I arrived in Detroit, Hugh White had already directed his
new industrial mission toward battling this point of view. His
strategy involved the building of an intimate relationship between
D.I.M. and four Episcopal parishes. Though all suburban, they
represented the whole social and economic spectrum of industrial
Detroit. In these four areas, called the "associated parishes," he
hoped to help the laity discover an industrially relevant theology
and mission, and also if possible to prick the churches into re-
newing themselves and becoming institutions dedicated to serving
the world. He had won support from their clergy and laity alike,
and with them had made hundreds of personal visits to members
of the congregations at their work, as well as leading several
stimulating discussion seminars in the parish halls. I joined him
in these tasks and continued the practice of regularly preaching in
the four churches as well. In one of them the group discussions
we organized, which followed the service, met with a warm and
enthusiastic response. In two churches we convened the unemployed to grapple with their predicaments during the 1958 recession.

All this was built on a foundation laid earlier, during several
years when the pastors and members of their congregations had
attended conferences at Parishfield, a lay training center outside
Detroit. Here they had come in contact with some of the most
exciting current theology imported from Europe, connecting the
church more vividly with a mission and ministry to the world.

We ourselves, and as a result of the work of Parishfield several
of the parish clergy, were committed to the theory of mission that
became popular after the Second World War. The church con-
sists of laymen who spend most of their lives working in secular
institutions. If they can be trained, energized, and supported in
their parishes, they can become effective lay ministers wherever
they work in the world. In order to achieve this goal our associated
parishes would have had to readjust their priorities to some extent,
so as to direct their energies primarily toward this training, in-
spirational, and supportive function. Groups specifically designed
to fulfill these roles would have to be created in the parishes and
the roster of those that perform mere maintenance functions reduced to the bone. The altar guild, for instance, would have to be
made as small and functional as possible. The conventional men's
club should be disbanded. The number of lay readers and servers
required, and the time demanded of them, should be minimized.

These are considerable changes. Yet we had reason to believe
that we might be at least partially successful. Hugh had been three
years on the Parishfield staff before coming into the city to start
D.I.M. He had contagious enthusiasm and a special gift of friendship which made his relationship with his fellow clergy and people
generally intense, personal, and consuming. He was well known in
the diocese and had evolved this plan in consultation with the
clergy of the parishes involved and many others. These clergy were
not only deeply interested in our work but were also our colleagues
in it, and together we hoped, at least in part, to redirect the orientation of the parishes toward the world of industry and enrich
their life through secular involvement.

This common concern gave birth to, and was nurtured in, a
theological study group that began before I arrived in Detroit and
met during all the time I was there. Though this circle included
several not in the associated parishes, through the years together
we found insight, mutual support, and friendship. But in spite of
the enthusiasm kindled by the plan and the success with seminars

and discussions in the parish halls, the clergy found that to become involved in industry was far from easy. Even the first leap
across the chasm between the parish and industry, when burdened
with parochial responsibilities, proved more difficult than had at
first been imagined.

One minister had worked in a large Detroit steel mill before
doing graduate work and returning to an inner city church. "It's
no use," he said when I suggested a visit to the union hall he had
previously frequented. "I'm out of touch. Since I've been back in
Detroit as a minister I've intended to go down to the local, but
I just don't have time. Now I've been away so long I'd feel strange
about going. I'm afraid they've forgotten me, or anyway I'd be out
of place."

Two others from outlying towns insisted that a parish minister
could visit men regularly at work and build up a consistent relationship with the industries in the parish. My words of caution
about the difficulties they would face did not dampen their enthusiasm, but in both cases their efforts survived only a few months
before they accepted calls to other parts of the country.

Still another pastor, one of our closest friends, recounted his difficulty in keeping up with the work situation of his parishioners.
During a rail strike he prayed for a settlement of the strike and
for those involved in it. He even mentioned by name a member
of his congregation who was a railroad employee. At the church
door after the service the man thanked him for the prayer, but
pointed out that his company was one of the few not on strike.

THEOLOGICAL FEEDBACK

This parish experience, beginning with my very first days in
Detroit, forcibly educated me in a number of important respects.
I learned that in the industrial setting most laymen find their
faith unintelligible in the context of the world of work. In these
parishes I became intensely aware of the difficulty of understanding

the gospel even within the walls of the church. At a conference at Parishfield, for instance, certain members of one congregation had begun to suspect that a true Christian must either leave the field of business or resign himself to failure. Soon after this the pastor suggested that I preach on the question, "Can a man be a Christian and successful in business?"

My sermon began with some examples of the kinds of real moral dilemmas that businessmen have to face. From this I moved into an exposition of *justification by faith*. I claimed that a successful businessman could of course be a Christian because he, like the rest of us, could admit his failings, trust in God's forgiveness, and try to make more rather than less responsible decisions. Christians, I argued, are those who affirm these things and not those who merely live by a certain moral code or have a set of solutions for particular moral problems.

The discussion of the sermon that followed the service showed that the congregation was familiar with the words of the doctrine but could not understand or accept it. Their position might be stated in these terms: Christianity is fundamentally a set of rules. A person who follows these rules with a certain amount of success is a Christian and a good man. If the rules are interpreted loosely, most of us can be considered Christian. On the other hand, if they are interpreted strictly many businessmen will be outside the Christian pale because of the practices that business demands. In the discussion these laymen insisted that "God can't keep forgiving if we do the same thing again and again."

"We at least have to be improving a little for Him to forgive us."

"No, we can't be perfect, but we can get better little by little."

They found justification by faith difficult because they could not believe in the combination of men so morally corrupt and a God so forgiving. Their view of man too exalted; their view of God too modest. The most telling comment was one man's remark that in my sermon I should not have just stated the moral dilemmas, but also suggested the Christian solution for them.

"Then the sermon might really do some good," he said. This comment would indicate that the speaker could not accept my argument (my position at the time) that there is no solution for the moral ambiguities of life; that God forgives us in any case, and that Christian ethics cannot give solutions to concrete moral dilemmas. My attempt to help men seriously to scrutinize the gospel and relate it to the world seemed mostly to make them feel guilty. They heard the judgment but not the grace.

This problem confronted us in other parish groups as well. At the largest of the associated parishes I regularly met with a group of men from business and industry. Perhaps lack of time or other pressures kept them away, but none of the top managers of the big corporations participated in the groups. Instead, the membership consisted of salesmen, independent businessmen, professionals, middle managers, and in one or two cases presidents of very small companies. At our monthly meeting we discussed case studies, talked about books we had read on theology or social criticism, and rubbed ideas together with visiting speakers. Several times we organized weekends for intensive Bible study and discussion. At one of these, Professor Tom Green from Michigan State University served as lecturer and resource person. He brilliantly analyzed the breakdown of community in American society. His description of cynicism, epicureanism, and stoicism as the traditional responses to the breaking up of community seemed to meet the men where they were and led to vigorous discussion and real involvement. But in his third lecture Tom tried to expound the Christian faith in terms of human predicament in a society of disintegrating community. Introducing certain new terms, including sin, judgment, and creatureliness, he made an extremely impressive theological statement.

The group however stood back, baffled. They could not really see how the gospel as he expounded it met the questions they had discussed in the first two sessions. We wallowed in abstractions until someone asked whether it was moral to sell a car to someone you knew could not afford it, or whether it was right to push $250,000 worth of Edsel cars on dealers when you knew they would have to sell them to bad risks. The group came alive when these issues were mentioned and demanded a Christian answer to them. They wanted to know the right solution. Tom then explained, as I had in my sermon on justification, that he could not give them the "right solution"—that there might seem to be no right solution —but in that they made the decision in good faith, they could be confident in God's forgiveness.

But here again the communications gap proved unbridgeable. Their genuine anxiety, it seemed, could only be met by the offer of practical solutions or at least the assurance that their decisions were right. Tom could only talk in terms of motives and forgiveness.

A most frustrating conference for myself was one at Parishfield in which the same group wrestled with the social responsibility of corporations. During the first half of the weekend we were provoked into intense involvement by a case study, a *Harvard Business Review* article, and a lecture on some of Peter Drucker's ideas. In the latter part of the conference we brought to bear both biblical and theological resources on the questions just discussed. The bubbling of discussion with which all the sessions overflowed gave me the feeling we had begun to communicate on every level. A week later one of the most articulate participants gave an informal report on the conference to a group at the church. His colorful and detailed description of the first part of the weekend delighted me, as did his conclusion that the experience had been worthwhile. But since fully half the conference had been spent on theological issues, with some sense of progress and understanding, his complete silence about the weekend's theological content left me stunned.

Our difficulties in connecting basic Christian ideas and the industrial situation apparently did not negate the value of this group to its members. For three years I participated with ten to fifteen men meeting each month and engaging in spirited and earnest conversation. At times I suspect we succeeded in producing a glimmer of light on the industrial relevance of Christianity; I know they were often stimulated by our analyses of industrial life, and their response showed clearly that the opportunity to talk together served an important pastoral function. For them the group proved the church's concern for them in their work. Unfortunately, however, only a small core of men stayed with the group all during the three years I was with it. The majority attended a few times or retired after participating for a year. With new faces constantly joining the circle, we found ourselves repeatedly having to go over the same ground. This made forward movement impossible. Nevertheless, the very existence of the group deserves notice because it indicates a thirst for meaning in life beyond what society generally offers. It was the convener of this group who reminded me that in asking men to consider Christianity seriously in their daily work we were facing them with a most threatening proposition.

"Think of the man," he said, "who has a good job with bright prospects, a nice house in this expensive suburb, family responsibilities, and a sizable debt. He's enjoying life and has great hopes for the future so long as nobody rocks the boat. Is he going to go looking for trouble, and enter seriously into conversation with a group he suspects are asking questions about the rightness of his own goals and values—about the system in which all his hopes for the future lie?"

The thirst for meaning, at least for a while, seemed great enough to drive men to this risk.

PROBLEMS AND BACKLASH

Not only did the clergy of the associated parishes find it almost impossible to leap across the chasm and regularly visit the world of industry, but equally they found it extremely difficult to reorient their parishes toward ministry to the world beyond their walls.

Commitment on their part was not lacking, but the pressures in the parishes for the *status quo* proved so much greater than they had expected that they wondered whether successful change was even possible. During a session with the clergy of the associated parishes, one of the pastors demonstrated the difficult nature of our basic D.I.M. proposal to adjust church priorities to the new horizon. He covered a blackboard with a list of activities and responsibilities in his own parish directed toward parish maintenance. When he finally came to mission and ministry to the world, he had only two inches of space left in the lower righthand corner of the board. He thus graphically showed that at least 90 per cent of these activities were directed toward maintenance of the parish. This left not more than 10 per cent of its time and energy for mission and ministry to the world, which we argued were the *raison d'être* of the church. This minister was not prepared to stir up the wave of opposition he was convinced would be aroused by such a radical policy as we proposed. Other clergy felt that they could do no more than talk about a revolution in city or suburban parish. Some even launched a really new policy, only to give it up when opposition developed.

It may indeed be impossible in most situations for any but the most gifted minister to make a genuine, forward-looking change in the traditional parish program without inviting civil war in his domain. Most parishes I can think of that have successfully developed new patterns of parish life in this country have been inner city parishes, whose original congregations have largely moved away or been driven out when the new policy began. Our best achievements lay in the development of programs with limited objectives such as the sermon discussion groups, the meetings with the unemployed, and the industrial study group for businessmen, mentioned above. These programs flourished only with a tremendous investment of time and energy on Hugh's part and my own. But instead of reorienting the life of the parish as we had hoped, they seemed rather to add new programs which left the parish basically unchanged, and which might not long survive the removal of our leadership.

This lack of success in helping the four associated parishes develop a new model of parish life dampened some of the enthusiasm that might otherwise have caught hold of the clergy of the area beyond our circle of close friends. I asked a young assistant minister his opinion of the general attitude of the clergy in the area toward D.I.M.

"Most of the time," he answered, "they don't think about it at all. They're absorbed in other things and haven't really time for it. But when they do think of it, as far as I've observed, it's almost with the feeling, 'I really don't understand what they're doing.' The only time they hear from you is when you ask them for money and send them a letter and a nice little brochure." This was a presentation of D.I.M. of which we had sent out some hundreds of copies to clergy of the region beyond those we could contact personally. Hugh, of course, was a native son.

"Do you think they read the brochure and get anything out of it?" I asked.

"I gave it five minutes. My rector says he isn't against D.I.M., but there are ten other good causes whose appeals clutter his desk. He just hasn't time to take a very great interest. I'm favorably disposed toward it myself, but I feel much the same way he does. I felt closer to industrial mission and more enthusiastic when I was in seminary."

This curate had visited us while he was still in seminary and had talked with us several times since coming to Detroit. I judged that the change from his former enthusiasm to his new indifference sprang from his new responsibilities. Since he was on a parish staff, his work and experience were within the church. D.I.M.'s difficulties in developing means to revitalize parish life removed the mission from the locus of his greatest concern. Our work with industry drew us into a universe far removed from his interests.

Overt hostility and skepticism joined with indifference to complete the ecclesiastical backlash. More typically, the clergy of Detroit shared neither our point of view nor our frustrations. But they extended to us invitations to speak and sometimes helped us. For instance, on one occasion I was asked to address a businessman's lunch club in a downtown church on D.I.M. Enough parish groups had responded positively to my presentations to leave me unprepared for the reaction that followed. I had hardly finished my talk before an old man stood up and strongly recommended that the factories in Detroit have Good Friday services in them. He was convinced it was possible. He then remarked that there was a vice-president of a corporation in the city who had a cross hanging on his office wall; this seemed to him a wonderful thing, and he was sure it was true because he had made the cross with his own hands.

An almost inarticulate hostile comment followed from the far end of the table. After this an old lawyer spoke, emotionally warning that the church should never take a stand or meddle in issues relating to industry. He urged that the church's proper function is to serve as an inspiration in general ways and not get involved in affairs of the world. The meeting ended with the rector's pronouncement that the work of the church should be done through the institutional parish. There, he said, is where men must be ministered to and children nurtured. Though he admitted D.I.M. might help the parish by bringing its clergy information about life in industry, his attitude toward this was, he said, open-minded but skeptical.

The invitations to speak to church groups continued to come in, however, and a considerable fraction of our time was spent talking to church conferences, consulting with church committees, and meeting with visitors from churches out of town and out of the country. At certain periods in fact Hugh found it hard to free himself enough from church involvements to spend more than a token amount of time in industry. As far as we could see, however, our efforts and those of our friends left the church basically untouched.

At a church convention in Detroit the preoccupation of the meeting with its organization, its growth, and its budgets gave no hint that the church had any awareness of its failure to communicate its message to the world outside.

I found myself thinking of the church as a giant ocean liner, full of people, churning through the mid-Atlantic swells. The mass of passengers were enjoying themselves eating, drinking, engaging in deck games or dancing. The crew was divided up between those who waited on the passengers and those laboring in the engine room to drive the ship at greater and greater speeds. Below decks a mere handful of men worked desperately, manning the pumps and wrestling to fasten the watertight doors, for—strangely—there was a hole in the ship's side, and, though still small, it was growing larger. Occasionally the ship's officers or passengers would invite someone struggling with the inrushing water to describe its progress. This added interest to what was otherwise a thoroughly routine trip. In fact, a few of the passengers found these reports so interesting that they made up to the crew members the wages that had been withheld from them since they abandoned their normal duties of waiting on the passengers to work the pumps. But generally speaking, life on shipboard was so engrossing, and the ship was making such good time, that very few on board took more than passing interest in the fact that every mile saw it sinking lower and lower into the sea.

Others, too, were finding the institutional church impervious to the changes we urged. The decade preceding my experience in Detroit had seen the arrival in the diocese of an exceedingly promising group of young clergy. They came armed with the best insights of Reinhold and Richard Niebuhr, Paul Tillich, and such brilliant Episcopal seminary teachers as Massey Shepherd, Reuel Howe, and Clif Stanley. They truly felt they had some answers, and were determined to make worship in their parishes something real and relevant, and to stir their people to carry out effectively the church's mission to the world. In Parishfield they found a rallying point. Their discussions projected an air of excitement, for in these ideas they believed lay the hope of the church, and of the world.

After ten years, several of the men had left the diocese. Those who remained no longer strode through their parishes with the same vigor; instead they found themselves plodding. Their best ideas brought dubious results. Their sense of direction became uncertain. The air of excitement had vanished. The church at large seemed to take little interest in their mission. They complained of feeling trapped.

"We should be just as persistent and patient in our work with the parishes as we are in our work with industry," Hugh repeated again and again in our moments of discouragement.

Nevertheless, our work with the associated parishes began to peter out. Checking one Wednesday on the arrangements for my scheduled preaching the next Sunday, I was told that since it was "theological education Sunday" I was not to preach. This was the fourth of five previously scheduled preaching engagements at that church to be canceled. I did not really feel that the pastor was against my preaching, but rather that in his eyes D.I.M. represented an optional extra of such slight importance in the life of the parish that other things took priority over it.

On Christmas Eve I assisted at the crowded service at another of the four churches. The carols were moving, the liturgy beautiful, and the whole mood of the church communicated the meaning and joy of the Christmas message. This was almost the rector's last service before shifting to another suburb; his departure meant for the parish the end of an era.

I felt a little depressed. D.I.M. had been associated with the parish for four years. In this time, it seemed to me, we had built nothing of enduring value. Although some of the congregation were friendly, I knew none very well and few in terms of their work. I did not feel that any of them had become particularly excited about the mission or involved in it. Our study program at this particular church had certainly not been a great success. Our sermon discussions had failed to win much interest in the congregation. In fact, with the rector's departure it seemed that D.I.M. had very little to show for four years of association.

A year later we unmistakably reached the end of the line with that parish. The new rector had been installed for several months, and I had talked with him at length. I gave the annual report on D.I.M. to the vestry and described (interestingly I hoped) the progress we had made in the past year, concluding with an appeal for suggestions as to ways in which D.I.M. and the parish could work together. Discussion followed.

Only one vestryman made any articulate comments about D.I.M. He commended it for its growth and development and expressed surprise that we should report to the vestry. The parish, so far as he knew, had contributed nothing to help the mission, financially or otherwise.

No one on the vestry admitted knowing anything about the association with D.I.M. except that I visited the parish once a month to preach or to participate in the service. Someone did say that three men previously on the vestry did know something about it. But no one could think of anything significant that we could do together. In conclusion we agreed that the parish should remain friendly with D.I.M. and consider us as a resource when study courses relating to our interests were being planned. A vestryman who had been described to me as bitterly opposed to our work said nothing during the discussion. The new rector also was silent.

This discussion seemed right, as it merely ratified what had happened. In the beginning the parish association was a joint venture between the clergy and the D.I.M. staff. Hugh and I preached and led discussion groups in the parish and the parish clergy came with us to visit men in industry. But we could not press further. The parish clergy generally found they were too harried for time and too uncomfortable in industry to continue making visits on their own. Although initially we shared a commitment to renew the parishes for ministry to the world, we gradually discovered that this goal was either impossible, or perhaps in some cases more costly than the clergy felt they could afford. Having come to this decision they found themselves less than enthusiastic about our role as reformers. They might justly have said (though as far as I know they never did), "If you really want to renew a parish, why don't you become pastor of one yourself and try?"

On our part we could not rejoice in the feeling that our role as a resource to help the parish discover a ministry in the world had been transmuted to that of assistants in running not-so-extraordinary church programs. Honesty and realism helped us recognize that their primary interest probably had to be in parish and neighborhood while ours was properly in industry. When presently the parish association was dissolved, however, other members of the D.I.M. staff evolved mutually satisfactory programs with a variety of parishes, convening men from particular occupations for a set number of discussions. Such meetings were not intended to renew the parishes, but to arm individuals for their life in industry as Christians.

THE CHURCH INSTITUTIONAL

Thus we can hardly claim to have generally renewed the laity in the associated parishes. Nor, as it turned out, did we succeed in bringing to a new form of life the churches to which they belonged.

Few would directly challenge the assertion that the Church exists to serve the world. Instead, the idea was subtly emasculated, with a small "but" placed after it, and the following words: ". . . in order to serve the world the church must first of all exist." Or "be strong in itself." And this opens the door wide for absorption in self-serving activities, cautious protectiveness, and drives for denominational aggrandizement. Perhaps we needed to be unreasonable and shout, "The church's business is not to preserve its

own life first, so that it can serve, but rather to serve even at the
risk of its life." It may be that a church can serve best by throwing
its own safety and hopes of statistical growth to the winds. Perhaps only by such a death can a true resurrection take place.

But probably renewal of the churches along the lines of our
hopes was simply not in the cards. Some of the prophetic critics
whose writings began to invade the bookstalls in the late fifties
seem to feel this way. Gibson Winter, for instance, in his *Suburban
Captivity of the Church*, suggests that the local parish in its
present form, because of its exclusive class, denominational, and
racial character, offers an inadequate platform for the church's
true mission and ministry of reconciliation. Peter Berger has gone
further in asserting that the life of the typical local parish actually
inhibits the hearing of the Word of God and obstructs Christian
obedience. Prophets like these seemed to be saying, "For the
parish the time is too late for renewal. The more it grows in its
present form, the more harm it does to the cause of Christ."

Not a prophet but a sociologist illuminated starkly for me the
nature of the church's institutional predicament. Gerhard Lenski's
book, *The Religious Factor*, summarizes a Detroit area study in
which hundreds of people were interviewed about the effects of
their religious beliefs on their attitudes toward work, politics, eco-
nomics, family life, and education. First of all, the evidence suggests that contemporary prophets have been wrong in predicting
that our recent religious boom must be followed by a bust. The
churches according to Lenski will increase in size and strength,
and their vigor continue for some time to come. But this growth
does not necessarily involve a return to God or an increase in
faith, but rather seems linked with certain sociological trends. The
structure of American society is changing so as to reduce the
relative size of the poor and alienated elements in the population
least involved in the churches, and to increase the size of the
middle-class groups which have traditionally been most involved.
Furthermore, the theological and transcendental elements in the

life of religious groups seem to be fading. While the churches grow, Christianity declines, and a significant revival appears on the surface unlikely.

Next, Lenski denies the claim of so many of us that religion does not significantly influence the daily lives of the masses of people in Detroit. Indeed, he goes still further and argues that, indirectly, religion makes an impact on all institutions in the community. But under scrutiny this influence appears not quite what we would expect, and less than we might hope. Thus according to this writer, membership in one of the Protestant bodies tends to produce men who differ from those in other religious groups. But the Protestant mentality he describes appears far more akin to the spirit of capitalism than to the spirit of Christ.

Finally and most important, Lenski stresses that the influences of religion are carried far more by way of the culture of the four religious subcommunities (Protestant, Catholic, Jewish, Negro) than through sermons preached or leadership exercised by the clergy. Although religiously identified, the "communities of faith" are more significantly cultural, social, and communal groups. So tangential do theological considerations seem in church affairs that I myself sometimes wonder whether an irrefutable proof that the gospel was fraudulent (cf. the imaginary letter in Peter L. Berger's book Precarious Vision) would make the slightest difference to the life and vigor of the church. Lenski's book implies that it might not.

The religious subcommunities are very conservative, in any case. Although they do change, this usually happens unconsciously or with a belief that the change is a return to traditional ways of doing things. In our rapidly shifting society, religious tradition is often seen as the one stable point of reference to give a sense of security, and in that same fluid, mass society men need stable and secure personal relationships. They need to belong to primary groups of people like themselves with whom they can relax—of whom they know what to expect and with whom some of the stresses and strains of the hurly-burly of industrial life are reduced.

The church in America has traditionally served as this kind of a sanctuary. Moreover, in the vastness of our cities men need status. They need to belong where their worth will be recognized. Or, if their membership in a group itself implies status, so much the better. This, too, is a need the church has often been able to satisfy.

The prophets are not primarily concerned with these functions of the church, which sometimes work directly against the gospel. Yet though they are often unverbalized and even unrecognized, these functions are in many cases more powerful than any theological statement the minister can make. Our attempts to renew the churches by means of a new theology, better preaching, Bible study, and discussion groups have hardly met with sensational success.

No wonder.

In his later works, Søren Kierkegaard more and more explicitly castigated the Danish Church for imagining itself to be the Church Triumphant instead of the Church Militant here on earth. But at no point could the church in his day respond creatively to his challenge. After a century of oblivion Kierkegaard has been rediscovered, and is more widely read, discussed, and admired now than in his own time. But the church seems just as incapable today as in Kierkegaard's time of acting as the Church Militant. Perhaps we should not expect it ever to be the Church Militant. Perhaps the best it can be is the Church Institutional.

Nevertheless, although not militant itself, perhaps it can be a seedbed for militant Christians who will witness in the world in obedience to God's will—with, or often without, the church's blessing. In fact, this is how the church has functioned historically. In the latter years of the nineteenth century, churches in England were a long way from endorsing the labor movement. But its Methodist laymen and lay preachers provided a large part of the dedication and leadership that brought the labor movement to recognition. And these Methodists in many cases were read out of the church for their "radical" stand. The Episcopal League for Industrial Democracy—not the church as an institution—supported the labor movement in the twenties and thirties in America. A little later, in Germany, the comparatively small Confessing Church rather than the bulk of German Christians opposed the Nazis.

In the civil rights struggle in America today, in spite of their official pronouncements in favor of integration, only a small fraction of existing churches are vividly engaged in the struggle. Even on such an obvious evil as slavery, the church in this country never took a militant stand until the Civil War. And when a stand was taken, the church split. Nevertheless, a large number of the early Abolitionists were Christian ministers and devout laymen. Without their passion and martyrdom, the Abolitionist movement might never have become a power. And their witness, though more often than not repudiated by it at the time, was the glory of the church.

Although Abolitionist Wendell Phillips once referred to the church as the "synagogue of Satan" because of its general support of slavery, he understood its limitations better than many of us today.

The pulpit, for instance [he said], has a sphere of its own. It is too busy getting men to heaven to concern itself with worldly duties and obligations. And when it tries to direct the parish in political and social ways, it is baffled by the fact that among its supporters are men of all parties and of all social grades ready to take offense at any word which relates to their earthly pursuits or interests, and spoken in tone of criticism or rebuke.

As the minister's settlements and salary depend upon the unity and good-will of the people he preaches to, he cannot fairly be expected, save in exceptional and special cases, to antagonize his flock. If all clergymen were like Paul, or Luther, or Wesley, they might give, not take orders. But as the average clergyman is an average man he will be bound by average conditions.*

* Oscar Sherwin, *Prophet of Liberty: Wendell Phillips* (New York: Bookman Associates, 1958).

This understanding of the limits of the Church Institutional can save us from bitterness and despair at the prospect of its standing either on the sidelines or on the wrong side of most revolutions. The notion of the Church Institutional as the seedbed producing militant reformers, radicals, witnesses in each generation enables us to rejoice. But to produce such men for the industrial centers of our society, Christians need to discover a more powerful and appropriate interpretation of the faith and a more industrially intelligible rendering of its social ethic.

IV
THE WAY AHEAD

♦ ♦ ♦ ♦

SEVEN

❦❦❦❦❦❦❦

LEADERS CONVENE

"THE UNFAITH OF MEN is not so much revealed by their blasphemy or their unwillingness to name the name of God and to participate in the cultic rites, as it is shown in their lack of deep commitment to anything or any value beyond themselves. When D.I.M. searches with men to discover their ultimate values and commitments, we are engaging in a prophetic and critical task calling them to a faith commitment and out of their empty and unbelieving lives. When we discuss with men this deepest commitment, we are engaged with them in a religious exploration which is the heart of the Christian enterprise."

When Jesse made this point as part of our own ongoing discussion about the task of D.I.M., I responded, "Yes—a hundred times yes! But we have to go further. As Christians we see the basic issue not as between faith and unfaith but as between faith in God and idolatry. At least this is the primary issue in the Bible. We cannot say, 'It doesn't matter what a man believes so long as he has some kind of an ultimate commitment.' Ultimate commitment

can be given to white supremacy, success, the American industrial
system. We come to men in industry with *faith of a particular sort*
to commend. We may not know in what terms to commend it,
or how to allude to it at all in many situations, but our task is
to discover how it can be appropriately understood and communicated in industry. This has to be done through laymen. Otherwise our Christianity becomes a kind of esoteric gnosticism: FOR
CLERGYMEN ONLY."

We needed to find ways to discuss the content of Christianity
with laymen *in some appropriate manner*. We needed to enlist
them as colleagues committed to the task of theological discovery,
and to form fellowships of men concerned with the meaning and
the means of ethical action in industry.

This kind of commitment proved hard to come by. Tod, a
member of the Personnel Managers Group, was typical. After a
meeting in his plant with the union committee, he and two of his
staff questioned me about the relation between Christianity and
the meeting we had just attended. This led to a long discussion
about the concerns of D.I.M. As he drove me to my car, he confessed that he saw more clearly than before what I was trying to do.

"It's a very difficult job you have," he commented.

With managers in another big company, after several encounters
I felt I had become articulate if not eloquent in describing the
thrust of industrial mission. They usually seemed interested, intrigued, and not a bit hostile. Yet it did not seem to occur to them
that the mission could have any real importance to them. How?
How? How (I kept asking myself) can our friends be drawn into
seeing that my tasks is theirs as well?

From the earliest days in Detroit Hugh and I had hoped to find
a number of lay colleagues who would convene and lead discussion
groups of their associates without our being present. Such lay
leaders would not only extend D.I.M.'s influence far beyond the
limited time and energy of the staff, but also transform the mission into a lay movement indigenous to industry. We had in

mind to bring together, when the time was ripe, actual and
potential lay colleagues to build into a group of conscious leaders
who would meet regularly to share their progress and problems,
and to probe the meaning of our faith and of the mission to industry. The leaders in this group would see that they did not
stand alone but were linked to a larger movement. They would
find opportunities for mutual support. They would in a certain
sense become an industrial expression of the church.

We did not feel the time had come until the fall of 1960, after
Bob Batchelder joined the D.I.M. staff. Even then, fear of rejection made me a little nervous when I stopped in to invite the
convener of the Labor Forum to the first meetings of the Leaders
Group. I was relieved when he accepted and delighted when he
added, "I don't want to contribute to your church, but this work
is so important I want to contribute something to its financial
support."

One evening three weeks later, more than a dozen of us gathered
at the Batchelders' for dinner and discussion. Looking around the
room I could see that leaders were not cast in the same mold.
Some were plant managers, some blue-collar workers, some union
officials, and an engineer and a lawyer completed the group. Because of the class, racial, and political differences represented, the
conversation rollicked, with the men finding a certain exhilaration
in bouncing ideas off others from different or "hostile" camps.
When we came to focus on a plan for the group, we found agreement and support for our proposal that we should meet for dinner
and an evening four times a year to discuss the purposes and
meaning of industrial mission and report on the progress and
prospects of the groups in industry. This format proved so agree-
able to those present that we continued it for three years. As it
worked out, we even enriched our agenda to include occasional
discussion of issues such as industrial democracy, economic myths
and realities, civil rights, and visitors' reports from industrial
missions in other parts of the world.

In themselves the meetings were successful. But as means for developing a cadre of committed laymen who would lead groups of their associates in discussion for theological discovery and responsible action, they succeeded only partially. At the end of a year and a half, one man was actually convening and leading a group of his own. Six others who attended our leaders' meetings were convening groups; these were, however, led by members of the D.I.M. staff. As often as not, when with great effort we added a new group and new leader to our gatherings, one of the established groups would disintegrate. Some prospective leaders found that in spite of repeated attempts they could not manage to pull a group together at all. Thus our dream that D.I.M. could start a large number of groups led by laymen who met with us as colleagues never materialized. We showed that it was possible for groups to exist, but we failed to prove that they could become the basis of a practical strategy for D.I.M.

With blue-collar workers the source of difficulty stood out clearly. Jesse and Jim, at least, felt that when a worker developed the courage, initiative, sense of leadership, and responsibility to be an effective lay leader on the production line, he also found that he had just the qualities for a better, middle-class type of job. In American society working-class life and production-line labor are so lacking in status and sense of integrity that it seemed doubtful whether we would ever find even a handful of men, capable of moving into the middle class, who would prefer to remain workers and lay leaders for Christ's sake. With managers our diagnosis was different. Those who had real leadership potential and expected to rise in their companies learned to keep their eye on power. The kind of activity we proposed offered little opportunity to enhance a promising manager's career. On the contrary, conspicuous involvement in D.I.M.'s groups could distract him from his job and possibly lead his superiors to look at him askance.

Behind these good reasons for the failure of our leaders to bring to life many groups in industry lurked the real cause. Our more fundamental failure was theological. We had won our leaders' friendship and awakened their interest, but had been unable to make compellingly clear what we and they were about. Even after a fairly prolonged evening's discussion with the D.I.M. staff, when they approached their associates at work to suggest founding a group their hearts wavered and their tongues stammered.

PUSHING FURTHER

If we and these leaders could develop an interpretation of the faith that would be simple, clear, and desperately relevant to the industrial situation, our strategy would be immeasurably advanced. With this task in mind we began the second phase of the Leaders Group. I had prepared an outline for a series of discussions focused on simple statements about life as seen in Christian perspective. These assertions I supported by biblical references, attaching to them some suggestions of their industrial relevance.

We launched this phase of the Leaders Group with a discussion of the claim that man is more than an economic animal. Among other things this might imply that he needs social relationships, which can only develop in somewhat stable settings. I argued that management and unions too often operate as if the nonmaterial needs of workers were unimportant. For instance, the practice of bumping workers around within the plant and moving managers around the country within a company seemed to ignore the human price of repeatedly uprooting the individual from his social context. In other cases, I contended, workers were given good pay and healthy working conditions but denied the opportunity to grow, to be responsible, and to be treated with respect.

The discussion that followed was lively and intense. I had hoped the group would explore the differences between my assertion that man was more than an economic animal and the assumptions underlying some current industrial practices. But instead the discussion avoided reference to the general assertion and became fragmented, with debate raging over many examples and each group member reporting cases in which particular practices had paid off. Disappointment might have been avoided if we had begun rather with a reference to the practice of frequently moving workers and managers and had then, with strong chairmanship, pushed to an examination of the human assumptions underlying the practice. This might have led to a consideration both of the Christian understanding of man and of popular alternative views, and would also have indicated how different views of man's nature can lead to different industrial policies.

At another meeting of the leaders we discussed at length the kind of men needed in the world of industry today, relating what seems to be required by our social situation to traditional images of the Christian personality. We were stretching, in other words, toward a reinterpreted doctrine of vocation, and proposed that the Christian should be honest, reflective, willing to become involved, and free. Perhaps the Negro radical in the group felt we were devising another Boy Scout oath when he asked, "How can this kind of a new man emerge when society tends to produce men of quite a different sort?" He could not be convinced that the Christian faith as we had presented it thus far could produce personality types in significant numbers that could strongly resist contrary trends of society.

When I returned from vacation that year, I found that the group had dealt in my absence with another of my theses for discussion. The meeting had flopped and the rest of the staff seemed generally sour on further theological exploration along this line. Perhaps because I had not been present at the meeting, I felt both convinced that we could pursue theological discussion with the leaders and laden with ideas as to how to proceed. I proposed, for instance, that we spend an evening or even a series of evenings on a serious theological and sociological analysis of mission strategy, with presentations of the basic Christian faith and the "technician

mentality," based on Hugh White's book *Christians in a Technological Era.* This might include an outlining of the problem of
ethics in industry, where so often traditional moral rules seem
misleading or at best unhelpful. I thought we might invite Joseph
Fletcher, a professor at Episcopal Theological School in Cam-
bridge, to meet with the group and share his views as to where a
solution to the problem might be found. Or we might have an
explication by Paul van Buren on his ideas of secular Christianity.

None of these suggestions was adopted that year. "We mustn't
burden the leaders with our theological problems," Hugh warned,
and the rest of the staff seemed to agree.

Nevertheless, we continued to work with the leaders, and the
group survived for two years longer. On one occasion they were
challenged by a manager and union official from a small plant
which had been experimenting successfully with a style of participative management. Another evening, the group was enlarged to
hear and discuss the report of John Soleau, a seminary professor
who had taken a senior management course at Harvard Business
School. These and other meetings of the leaders raised significant
questions and, as meetings, could be called successful. A few of
them fizzled. One evening only six leaders managed to attend. Of
these, one had never come before, one had participated only once,
while a third came so rarely I could not remember his name.
Unluckily the three thoroughly initiated men present were among
the most taciturn of our membership. This small gathering of
comparative strangers predictably produced a well-mannered and
very subdued encounter. Perhaps the men present found it interesting; they can hardly have found it exciting or very much fun.

At one meeting an outburst by one of the managers confronted
us with a moment of truth, and made it for me the most significant
meeting of the series. Jesse had begun with a thoughtful and carefully written statement on "What D.I.M. Contributes to Industry," in which he claimed that the mission could enhance the
processes of reflection, communication, self-criticism, and respon-

sible action within corporations. When he finished, the responding
comments came slow and mild until one leader—a young manager
—stood up.

"The presentation was fine," he said. "I can't find anything to
disagree with. In fact I'd recommend its endorsement by the
Ladies' Aid." Frustration was written on his face as he continued.
"You see, it seems completely innocuous. It communicates no
sense of urgency. It isn't likely to arouse enthusiasm. The industrial mission is the one thing the church is doing that makes
real sense to me. It seems like the church's most relevant thrust.
But surely it must be more significant than this presentation
shows!"

I submitted that the sense of urgency and significance would
come if we explicitly stated what, because of our Christian outlook, we were for and what we were against in the present industrial system. Our theology, in other words, as directly applied.
But Jesse defended his original statement, first on the grounds that
he was not seeking controversy but rather assent and access to
industry from managers. Moreover, he ventured, the kind of sub-
stantial comments about industry that I proposed smacked of an
insensitive, authoritarian kind of theological pronouncement.
D.I.M., he felt, could skirt this pitfall by avoiding a particular
critique of industry and emphasizing the human processes noted
in his statement instead.

The evening ended. The leaders continued to meet through the
last year of the group's three-year life. But contrary to our original
hopes and in spite of individual exceptions, as a group they failed
to become a cadre of men who led group discussions with their
work associates; nor did they become articulate lay theologians or
colleagues fully committed with ourselves in the industrial mission.

The point raised by the frustrated and angry young manager
remained. It produced all kinds of echoes in my mind from conversations both later and earlier, and led next day to some perceptive comments by Gerald Jud, an executive of the United

Church of Christ who had been visiting at the time, and who brought into sharp focus one of the most baffling dilemmas for industrial missions. In our private conversation with Jud he urged, "Take seriously the complaint that D.I.M. lacks passion. It's important. People are hungry for passion. One of the reasons for Malcolm X's appeal is the great passion with which he speaks. Industrial mission is one of the areas of the church's ministry where passion about really critical issues ought to be appropriate and effective."

"One of our difficulties," I said, "is that industrial managers are often afraid of it, or at least of overt passion. If we threaten to introduce a note of passion into our discussions, some would be afraid they couldn't control it and would wonder if it would be a nuisance to the company."

"It has yet to be proven," Jud replied, "that management is prepared to offer you enough freedom to carry on the proper kind of discussions within industry. It may be that your discussion will have to take place outside. At present D.I.M. is a rather self-contained good work. Without passion, I wonder if it will ever develop into a growing, dynamic movement."

OUR DILEMMA

This comment brought to the foreground a basic dilemma facing D.I.M. and indeed every serious effort of the churches to engage secular society in dialogue. We needed to maintain an even course between seduction by society as it is and exclusion from the sources of power—between employment as chaplains to the *status quo* and the position of impotent aliens on the fringe of society. This dilemma constantly confronted us with the question of how much criticism of management or labor we could express, or even what could be said in honest appraisal without abruptly closing all doors and putting an end to our work. As to the deeper problem of how far a coercive situation really extends, and how wisely to approach it—indeed, the whole question of how far conscious human personality does in fact control the industrial process at all—on this question we all admitted ignorance as well as difference of opinion as to the facts. We did not know to what degree anyone could control the development of our industrial system, or to what extent it is controlled by its own irresistible logic. Clark Kerr and his collaborators in their book *Industrialism and Industrial Man* give the impression that our course is already largely set and that our task is to adjust to the coming social realities. A. A. Berle, on the other hand, writes not only as if we could determine the future shape of our industrial system, but as if in fact he himself had determined its present shape in several particulars.

Nor did we know to what extent we should attempt to help human nature adapt to the requirements of our industrial structures. Most people would argue perhaps that human nature can and should adapt to industrial life, with its high mobility, its destruction of the extended family, its urbanization, and the ever-increasing gross national product and rate of theological and social change. A few might take a more critical stance, admitting the malleability of human nature but insisting that the deprivation of certain human needs on a large scale may eventually lead to disastrous psychic upheavals. This outlook would stress the importance of shaping the industrial system to human needs in some respects, instead of bending human life to the demands of the industrial system.

As a staff we had discussed all these questions enough to make it evident that my views on them differed from those of my colleagues. Only when, at one of our regular staff sessions of study and discussion, I offered a carefully written Christian critique of our industrial system, did the dimensions of this difference become clear. They tended to be more affirmative toward the system; I, more critical. They were more fearful of exclusion from it—I, of seduction by it. In the discussion some of my colleagues indicated that they found my criticisms deeply antagonizing. They asked them-

selves whether I had enough appreciation of our system—whether
I was not perhaps bound by nineteenth-century prejudices.

Admittedly my constructive affirmations were not as colorful or
forceful as the critical aspect of the paper. Moreover, as one colleague observed, the argument was exceedingly compact, each point
resting on implied reasoning of considerable range. But as we
discussed it, two further points occurred to me.

1. To criticize our industrial system as we now find it is not
necessarily to condemn industrialism altogether. It is possible, I
was sure, to develop a reliable industrial society that operates
differently in some respects; Britain and Sweden, as well as Russia
and other Communist countries, have done so. If our system has
become an idol, therefore, this does not mean that industrialism
in itself is evil, and to say that wealth cannot save us does not
mean we should make poverty our ideal.

To suggest that our system ought to be modified so as to be
more consistent with the fullest human needs and hopes does not
mean it has not achieved great and wonderful things so far. It is
changing, of course, all the time. Indeed, the challenge facing us
might rather be seen in terms of the fact that we who have the
most highly developed industrialism and the greatest affluence can
afford to experiment with solutions to the problems our system has
brought with it.

2. Possibly (I thought) I did have more nineteenth-century
prejudices than other members of the D.I.M. staff. In fact, it
might be that I had altogether more of a nineteenth-century cast
of mind. It was true that I had read a good deal in the literature
and social criticism of the period, and in a sense this gave me the
advantage of a perspective outside contemporary culture from
which to view it. None are so blind (I sometimes irritably felt) as
those whose prejudices are identical with those of their contemporaries. Moreover, something in me contended obstinately that my
prejudices stemmed not merely from the nineteenth century, but
also in certain respects from a valid understanding of Christianity.

These differences with the rest of the staff became manifest in a succession of controversies at staff meetings. It was not that the whole staff had taken up arms against my point of view; yet I generally stood at one pole of the discussion, with one or another of my colleagues opposite and the rest joining my antagonist or sometimes remaining neutral. Though no one presented me with a carefully worked-out argument, my basic approach to Christian social ethics was really not shared by anyone on the staff and was under fire generally.

I felt rather alone in my concern to try to discuss explicitly with laymen the fundamental truths of Christianity, in terms vivid enough to have life and meaning, and keyed to the implacable conditions of our modern settings, without unfaithfulness to their basic import. I seemed alone also in wanting to challenge Paul van Buren's position and generally radical approach to theological truth, and in wanting to keep the size of staff and budget as low as possible until we had developed some extensive breakthroughs in industry. My personal relations with the staff were good, and these disputes were not bitter. But the sense of being the odd man out, time and again, left me sometimes going home angry and lonely and hating my colleague's opinions. It was pointed out, and I'm sure it is true, that such conflict can be very creative. I was certainly forced to sharpen and clarify my position because of the challenge. It may even have been important also for the staff to be confronted by my own kind of thinking. But the situation was not entirely comfortable.

The reality of the problem came home to me again when I tested our assumptions by raising a certain question with a group of managers and union people from the automobile industry at a weekend conference we had organized. I knew it was like waving a red rag in front of a bull, but I went ahead nevertheless.

"Is an eight-million-car year a good thing for the country?"

I had in mind the theory that there may be something incompatible between vast numbers of large motor cars and civilized

urban living. Traditionally successful urban living has depended
on a high density of population with a great variety of people,
activities, and resources in close proximity. This had made for
the possibility of grandeur, stimulation, and resources for every
taste within easy reach. But the automobile makes for dispersal.
People live in widely scattered locations. Centers of various activities move apart as if by centrifugal force. Centers and neighborhoods become separated from each other by wide boulevards, vast
parking spaces, and acre-eating expressways. In this sort of situation
one might argue that a rational course would involve studying the
nature, possibilities, and dynamics of urban living and the various
values enhanced and sacrificed by the universal use of big cars,
and then making some sort of attempt to adjust the volume of
vehicles to the best interests of society.

I suppose the response to my query might have been predicted.
"That's a silly question," said one manager, "—not worth talking
about."

"Why, the automobile companies have nothing to do with
that," claimed another. "We only make the cars the public demands."

"How can we have full employment if we don't keep increasing
our car sales?" asserted a third.

In their minds the question was not legitimate. They did not
want to discuss it or even think about it. The rightness of the
current goals of their industry must be assumed. The only question
for discussion was how best to achieve them.

I couldn't help remembering that in the Bible the existence of
God is never questioned; His existence is the Given upon which
all other thinking depends. When one of my colleagues said to
me privately afterward that my question had been unhelpful and
unfair, I'm sure he was reflecting the feeling of the managers and
union men as well as his own.

Thus in my way I knew well the frustration of the angry young
manager who had burst out at us about urgency and significance.

I had passion to spare, but fear of losing access or breaking up the relationships I had developed with men in industry had bottled up my feelings. The thought occurred to me again when I heard Malcolm Boyd address a civil rights group on the moral challenge of integration. Of course he spoke colorfully, immoderately, and dramatically. And the crowd loved it. Anyone not committed to integration—and some who were—might have found the address shocking. But there was something refreshing about it, for by his life and involvements he was able to convey a compelling sense of urgency about the issue.

Since I had known most of the leadership of the group longer than Malcolm had, I asked myself bluntly why he seemed the right person to speak there rather than myself. Part of the answer was that he had become one of the most publicized Episcopal priests in that diocese, if not in the country. This was not only because he was both colorful and extremely gifted, but also because he was controversial. He had taken strong positions on a number of issues, particularly integration. In fact, he had been more than outspoken; he had dramatically demonstrated by his prayer pilgrimage, sit-ins, and relationships that he was in dead earnest. Thus his words had an impact far beyond their face value. If he had become one of the best-known Episcopal priests, he was also certainly in some circles the most hated. Such a colorful and controversial figure gets a hearing.

As for me, although I had spoken out on the matter of racial justice, in most instances I felt that my position demanded extreme caution. Like anyone who feels things passionately, I often found being reserved and moderate difficult. There were angry comments about my sermon at a prominent suburban church on white-collar dishonesty; cries of rage at my statement for civil rights legislation in the press; and firm rejection in certain places because of pointed questions I asked.

Reacting to one of Ted Wickham's presentations, made during a visit from England, a labor lawyer asked him if it was not always necessary for the Church to be on the side of the *status quo*.

"For example," he asked, "would the church ever stand publicly against General Motors in a strike?" I think Ted denied the implication at the time. But he has suggested that an industrial mission must accept the basic power relationships as they are. And D.I.M. might be crippled if it *did* publicly stand against GM in one of its conflicts with the union.

A friend who had been actively involved in the work of D.I.M. for more than five years put the question to me in a personal way.

"Does the work of the mission result in any increase in the practice of so-called Judeo-Christian ethics in the ranks of either labor or management, beyond an occasional individual act of no general significance? The only areas where it is taken seriously is by people with a serious sense of dedication socially. These are few and far between.

"Can this work (of Industrial mission), however well intentioned personally, hope to free people from the shackles of political and social compulsions *unless* it is integrated with political and social currents of rebellion and dissent?"

Another close friend with whom I had shared my journals confronted me with the issue in a way I could not escape. "Whether you mean them to be so or not, your journals are a terrific indictment of both unions and management. The attack on unions is new to me. You have all these damning insights and convictions, but you don't express them. What use are they if you remain silent? You don't criticize, and probably you can't without becoming *persona non grata* in these places. Are you going to fall into the trap of so many other institutions and come to worship the organization and its growth regardless of what it's really doing? I doubt whether you're accomplishing much of anything as things are going. And the contradiction between what you believe and what you can say and do is castrating you as a man."

To both these friends I had to admit that we had not yet managed to bring about a significant increase in the practice of

Judeo-Christian ethics. But as far as we knew, neither had anyone else. In fact, within the churches as on our own staff great disagreements existed as to what the application of Judeo-Christian ethics in the industrial situation would mean. What we had been doing was to engage a considerable number of men in serious conversation, discovering a small number who were already trying to live by these ethics.

I countered the questions of both my friends by insisting that to stimulate thinking, ask questions, and engage in discussion really could change attitudes that would make a difference, even without an overt attack on the industrial system itself. In any case, I felt that a grand suicidal gesture of frontal attack might be no more effective than preaching chastity in a brothel. At the moment it may not be possible to do more in industry than keep alive small circles of discussion and concern.

This we had begun to do. And in spite of our difficulties I had seen men in response to these discussions act with a sense of freedom and responsibility. I suspected that, given time and continued effort, these circles of concern might grow and multiply and prove to be decisively significant.

EIGHT

❧❧❧❧❧❧❧

Mission is to the church what burning is to fire.
                                            —Emil Brunner

STYLE OF A MISSIONER

"WOULD YOU CONSIDER the possibility of coming to Boston to be director of the new Boston Industrial Mission?" It was the voice of an old friend on the long-distance phone. I knew by then, in June 1964, that an industrial mission was being formed in Boston, but had somehow managed to keep any thought of personal involvement in it from invading my mind. But now I could not escape; I was forced to evaluate my share of the work and my own life in Detroit and decide whether it should continue. I thought myself happy. Part of this came from a sense of achievement, part merely from having survived and from the process of coming to grips with vital human issues. I had been doing full-time industrial mission work for longer than anyone else in the country. I felt I knew something about what it involved and had developed a mode of operation and even the style of life required for it. Thus the

135

following elements I had identified as necessary and to some extent
made my own.

1. *Constant initiative.* Horst Symanowski describes himself as
the hound dog of Christ, sniffing out His presence in the industrial
world. Perhaps we are not seeking Christ so truly as human relationship, in which Christ may ultimately be found. Yet it requires
tireless concentration, brooding, imagination, search for means of
engagement with men; points of common interest, common humanity, and opportunities for conversation. A local pastor can wait
in the church for people to come to him. A missionary must take
the initiative and go to the people.

2. *Involvement.* Once men are touched, the missioner must become involved or even absorbed in their lives. He must see them
at work, at home, at recreation, and at political meetings. He must
make their experience his own as much as he possibly can. One
of the temptations of a big industrial mission staff is for its members
to become absorbed in their own circle, with correspondingly less
time, energy, and will to absorb themselves in the lives of the men
in industry. Another temptation is to become involved in the life
of the community apart from industry. This is easier than industrial
involvement, and it can be both absorbing and distracting.

3. *Genuine fondness for people.* Werner Pelz in his *Irreligious
Reflections on the Christian Church* writes forcefully that to love
a person is to want to be *with* them, to enjoy them, to be drawn to
them. It is far more than liking—not *less*, as so many try to make
out. The missioner must love the men he works with in this
strenuous sense. He must not only have good will toward them,
and a sympathetic understanding, but must actually like them,
enjoy being with them, feel fond of them. They must be his friends.

4. *Positive pleasure* in building up a network of relationships
within an industrial location. To become known and accepted in
industry for some reason gave me enormous satisfaction.

5. *Confidence.* The missioner must be convinced that he has
something to contribute to life in industry. He needs to be with-

out sense of apology toward the men he is with, in times of crisis
as well as during the lulls in activity. For a missioner this sureness—
almost arrogance—is a high virtue. And of course unless he is
correct in his assumption that he is contributing he cannot get
away with it for long.

6. *Sensitivity.* The missioner must be alert to signs of positive
response from the men he meets with and be prompt and un-
flagging in appropriate follow-up.

This was a personal list. Others would draw it up differently.
But where I felt I succeeded it was because I lived and worked according to this style, and where I failed it was partly in departing
from it.

This life style and involvement in industry that gave me such
a sense of satisfaction, even exhilaration, filled some of our close
friends and supporters among the clergy with concern. "Don't be
seduced by the drama, color, the excitement of the dynamic world
of labor and management," they would warn. "You must never
undervalue the hard, humdrum, unsensational work of the loyal,
indispensable parish priest." These well-meaning friends could see
the glamor of industrial mission. But they seemed not to feel the
cost. Even the drama and excitement of union meetings faded
after years of exposure and often became deadly dull. But especially,
we worked without the kinds of support that most parish priests
take for granted.

After spending a day with me in industry one local pastor commented on this difference. He described the satisfaction of being
needed and helping individuals in a myriad of pastoral relations—
the established role of leadership given him in the midst of the
church community and the weekly preaching and celebration of
Communion among his people, which gave order and sustenance
to his life.

"You have none of these things," he said, "and you spend a good
deal of your time in hostile surroundings, without status, and frequently misunderstood."

In another connection my colleague Jim Campbell made the distinction between the powerful and the powerless. The powerful are sought after. They can help people and are therefore in great demand. Accordingly a very powerful man becomes accustomed to relating to people in terms of their needs and his power. "What do you want?" is an attitude he is subconsciously conditioned to take in meeting other human beings. But the powerless are not sought after. They can do few favors. On the contrary, they are frequently forced to humble themselves and seek favors from the powerful.

The experience of a local pastor is in many ways that of power. As an industrial missioner I found myself among the powerless. I could do little for others. Few sought me out. Most of my contacts derived from my own initiative. My hope had been that in time I would be more or less sought after by people from industry, turning to me because of their interest in some concern of the mission. This hope was not fully realized. Although individuals and groups from industry did occasionally seek me out, far more opportunities, demands, and requests came through the welfare, political, and social channels of the city. Even in my work itself there seemed to be a constant pull away from involvement in the institutions of industry and toward neighborhood and community concerns. At one point, for instance, two out of three of the issues suggested for Labor Forum discussions were community rather than industrial problems. And to tell the truth, in these community situations I tended to feel more at ease. I had to fight off the temptation to become completely distracted from industry by this kind of involvement.

Some of the seductiveness of community problems came from the common expectation that these were concerns in which clergymen should be involved. In the community also (as opposed to industry), the soil was richer for the sort of human values in which Christianity has been traditionally interested. Not that industry excludes these values, but they are distinctly subordinated to the need to meet competition and to make money. Again, in the community even the clergyman belongs. He is a citizen like everyone else, and maybe even a leader. But in industry I was an outsider no one quite knew what to do with: a foreign body causing anxiety if not irritation.

But I was convinced I must continue to resist most of the blandishments of the seductive city. Otherwise I would quickly be drawn away from an industrial center of gravity toward the community. So I found myself turning my back on situations in the church and community, where I knew I could win acceptance, and setting my gaze on industry, where I was not really wanted. The place I made for myself and the friendships gained came slowly and in the course of many ego-shaking rejections. I sometimes felt during my years in Detroit that my personality was actually changing and becoming subdued. Although I had always been a fairly quiet person, even to myself I seemed earlier to have been more lively, somehow, more bubbling with enthusiasm, more free with laughter. And it seems reasonable that the experience of self-imposed loneliness as well as overt rejection and suffocating indifference might help to leach out of one the traits of vivacity and spontaneity. In excess, at any rate, such experiences do not increase exuberance. In this period I luckily discovered Muffy McKay who became my wife and whose companionship helped counter those trends in me mentioned here.

As industrial missioners, we not only floated between the churches and industry without strong membership or support from either, but suffered from occasional uncertainty about our role and anxiety as to the salability of our product. One of my colleagues used to ask, "What claim do we have on the people we meet in industry?" And he suggested two: loyalty to the Church if they were managers, and the social idealism they might have if they were union people.

I knew how my colleague felt, from experience in the church as well as in industry. At the lower end of the scale there would be an occasional piling up of negative response in the form of calls unanswered, appointments canceled, and low attendance at meetings, which was discouraging. At that point the question would be not "What claim do I have on these people?" but rather, "Do my friends in industry get enough from our contact to make it worth their while?" They should at least find their relationship with us stimulating, fun, and helpful in seeing more clearly the meaning of their lives and work. Moreover, they should be able to see that we care about them personally. I obviously failed to communicate this to the man who said one day that he didn't really give a damn about the people he knew at work, and that they cared little for him—and that I was no exception.

This reaction was unusual. More often men offered me genuine friendship. But we were confronted with the need to answer skeptics who challenged the conception or importance of industrial mission, or in some cases just could not understand it. These challenges sometimes took the form of such questions as "What is D.I.M. doing that the Harvard Business School doesn't do better?" or "What is so specially Christian about this work?" or "What precisely is your longe-range goal, and how do you expect to reach it?" We wrestled with these questions and argued about them, and usually spelled out the following three purposes for our work.

1. The most obvious was to learn from men in industry about their world, in order better to understand industrial life. We hoped to share this understanding with the churches. This purpose usually met with a warm response from both labor and management, for alert leaders often saw us as potential unpaid propagandists for their side. For us this was the role of the "listening church." It was valid up to a point, for indeed we had much to learn from the world of industry. But we also believed that Christianity had something to teach industry—something we hoped these men might be able to understand without having first to be converted and to become skilled theologians.

2. The second purpose of D.I.M. that we cited to the men in

industry was the hope that we might help them face personal problems relating to their work. The economic and industrial system is usually assumed to be immutable. But maybe within it we could help them become more successful and at ease with themselves. By their own choice, many of our discussions centered on individual problems or personal decisions in the industrial setting. And the discussions certainly encouraged and comforted some.

3. But the church has more than a word of comfort and encouragement to give. It has more than a pastoral-evangelical role. The third purpose we urged was that of stimulating serious discussion of our evolving industrial society. It was, we argued, in the best interests of the new society that is being produced by industrial progress to develop along lines consistent with the social insights of the Christian faith and not in opposition to them. The responsibility of the church through its industrial missioners is to identify these social insights and discuss with men in industry how they relate to the existing situation.

THEOLOGICAL EROSION

In this role our contribution had to be informed by human wisdom and industrial experience, but it was nevertheless primarily theological. We had to discover secular language and concepts through which to express the Christian faith—language which both communicated successfully in the industrial context and also made a significant difference. We had naïvely imagined that immersion in the world of industry would soon lead us to new theological discovery, and also draw us in a new and powerful way to prayer, Bible study, and worship. But in industry we found, rather, that the secular winds blew so hard that we were inhibited from any kind of direct theological discourse, and in our thinking were subject to a kind of erosion. Part of this sprang from the special environment of industry itself and the usual focus of attention of the men who live their lives there. Somewhere in his journals Charles Darwin describes how, through years of single-minded concentration on scientific matters, he lost his capacity to enjoy and appreciate drama, art, music, and poetry. It was as if in industry, we, like so many modern men, because of absorption in technological and external matters, had lost the capacity for consciousness of God, or for inwardness. Some have embraced Bonhoeffer's cryptic allusions and celebrated the loss of this faculty as "man's coming of age." Others have described it as his dehumanization. In any case, it seems beyond argument that those who have lost the faculty most completely will be least able to appreciate what they have lost.

Another part of the theological erosion we experienced came from the habitual attempt of the men we worked with to reduce the Christian faith to some easy formula. "Tell me in a nutshell what Christianity is," we were often asked, as though, having learned the Golden Rule or the Ten Commandments, our questioners would then not have to think very much more about it. It was as if the men wanted a kind of "new speak" theology, like the language devised by the tyrants in Orwell's *Nineteen Eighty-Four*. (This, the reader may remember, reduced the rich heritage of our tongue to a kind of basic English, which eliminated as much vocabulary as possible, made undesirable thoughts difficult, and destroyed all unnecessary nuances and shades of meaning. The object was to limit and stereotype thought and reduce human feeling and expression to as near the animal level as possible.)

The pressing question faced us: Should we rejoice in this loss of traditional dimensions of religious experience and celebrate it as a sign of man's coming of age, or judge it as a tragic deprivation and seek to rediscover faith in a personal God, the discipline of prayer, and the life of inwardness? The answer did not come clearly to the D.I.M. staff. Some of my colleagues tended to lean toward the first alternative. I tended toward the second. But the second course offers the steeper path, for it involves struggling against the climate of the times and opposing the opinions of most authorities on industry, many intellectual leaders of the day, and the tacit if not verbalized feelings of the vast majority of our contemporaries.

In any case we wholeheartedly agreed that a simple translation of traditional religious words into modern idiom would be inadequate—would not communicate anything to our friends in industry. Some kind of radical reinterpretation of our religious tradition was needed. In insisting on this, we were rejecting the notion that any theological formulation of religious experience can be final, and were asserting that the fundamental experience of grace may have to be couched in different terms and thought about through different concepts in each generation. In fact, since intellectual climate varies from place to place and time to time, to use the same words and concepts in one period that have been formulated in another is to betray the earlier formulation and to mean something different.

In other words the theological task parallels the mapmaker's. The latter tries on a flat surface to picture the sphere of the earth. Each type of projection presents certain parts of the globe with fair accuracy while wildly distorting others. The Mercator projection distorts the polar regions, but was highly useful in the days when sailing ships charted their voyages back and forth across the equator. In an age of jet flight across the poles, however, a conical or polar projection becomes necessary.

Just as every projection somewhat distorts geographical reality, so every theological interpretation distorts religious reality. The distortions of Augustine, for instance, proved less troublesome to Europeans in the Dark Ages than the distortions of Origen. The distortions of Calvin somehow related better to the emerging capitalist states of northern Europe than the distortions of Aquinas. In his book The Rise of Rationalism, W. E. H. Lecky brilliantly describes the predicament we found as theologians in industrial Detroit.

The success of any opinion depended much less upon the force of its arguments, or upon the ability of its advocates, than upon the predisposition of society to receive it, and that predisposition resulted from the intellectual type of the age.

. . . The pressure of the general intellectual influences of the time determines the predispositions which ultimately regulate the details of belief: and though all men do not yield to that pressure with the same facility, *all large bodies are at last controlled.* A change of speculative opinions does not imply an increase of the data upon which those opinions rest, but a change of the habits of thought and mind which they reflect. Definite arguments are the symptoms and pretexts, but seldom the causes of change. They derive their force and efficacy from their conformity with the mental habits of those to whom they are addressed. Reasoning which in one age would make no impression whatever, in the next age is received with enthusiastic applause.

. . . It is impossible to lay down a railway without creating an intellectual influence. It is probable that Watt and Stephenson will eventually modify the opinions of mankind almost as profoundly as Luther or Voltaire.

If these views be correct, they establish at once a broad distinction between the province of the theologian and that of the historian of opinions. The first confines his attention to the truth or falsehood of particular doctrines, which he ascertains by examining the arguments upon which they rest; the second should endeavor to trace the causes of the rise and fall of those doctrines which are to be found in the general intellectual condition of the age.

. . . frequently civilization makes opinions that are opposed to it simply obsolete. They perish by indifference, not by controversy. They are relegated to the dim twilight land that surrounds every living faith; the land not of death, but of the shadow of death; the land of the unrealized and the inoperative.*

REINTERPRETATION AND RELEVANCE

In developing a theological interpretation, then, our problem was not primarily that men found traditional theology incredible, but they found it irrelevant and unnecessary in their day-to-day life and work, and it was perishing by disuse. Our task was to discover an understanding of the faith that would offer a compelling prom-

* Pp. vi–xxi *passim.* (London: Longmans, Green, and Co., 1910).

ise of a more significant life and a more meaningful society than
the alternative visions current in society at present. But in striving
to speak relevantly to social realities and win approval, the danger
was that we would lose touch with the religious realities in which
our theology was based. Inevitably, it seemed, we began our attempts at reinterpretation at the point of most men's greatest
concern.

"What does it mean to be a Christian at work?" asked one man.
"I work in a drafting office, and the only point I see where religion
is relevant is when I'm talking to people at the coffee machine.
And then I'm not working but goofing off."

"My job as steward prevents me from being a Christian," said
another.

"Christianity and business success are incompatible," claimed a
man who had somehow failed to embrace either.

In hundreds of individual conversations and scores of group discussions we scrutinized one insoluble moral dilemma after another.
These left me feeling that, while involvement in life repeatedly
requires the sacrifice of one value for another, the real problem
lay not in the necessity for compromise but in the causes back of
these particular compromises—in the fears and anxieties that so
beset men that they dare not do what they think is right, or even
be the persons they really are. Often fear of not receiving a promotion shackles men more subtly and tightly than fear of dismissal. The word of freedom these men needed to hear was difficult
to speak. We tried to pronounce it, in two ways chiefly. We expounded on justification by faith, and we explained that Christ
has so broken the Powers of the world that they need not enslave
us, and by recognizing this we can live with the freedom of those
whose future lies elsewhere.

One man told us of a time when he was made part of a small
management team on special assignment in an outlying plant of
a big company. The plant management did not realize that this
team was reporting directly to top corporate management and so

treated them with suspicion, not allowing them use of the management dining room or the management parking lot, or other symbols of prestige within the plant community. The managers with whom they talked were guarded, barely courteous, and generally treated them as outcasts. But the members of the team moved through this frigid atmosphere with a certain lightness and nonchalance. They were convinced that the plant management was sick and on its way out. The vice-president who had given them the special assignment had the right ideas, according to which they were to help reorganize the company. They might be outcasts at the moment, with neither power nor status, but the time would come when their power would become known.

Our friend suggested this as a parable of Christian freedom. Theoretically, a manager without a vice-president behind him can live with the same freedom and act with the same confidence because of his faith in Jesus Christ. Although we were able to win admission from men that they wished this might be so, in few cases did it become so. I am haunted by the thought that a few dramatic demonstrations of the reality of this freedom on my own part might have convinced more people than any verbal pronouncement.

At one point we described the stance of the Christian in industry in more extensive terms. It might be characterized, we said, by the following:

1. *Faith.* We must believe that God's grace and judgment are at work in every industrial situation, and we must try to perceive and point this out actively. Unanswered: How can such service be actively identified?

2. *Involvement.* Just as Christ involved Himself in the depth of human life, to follow Him and find Him we too must become involved and carry responsibility in the world.

3. *Reflection.* Though the major concern of men in industry must be technical means, this must not be their exclusive concern.

It is crucial that they take time to think deeply about the purpose and meaning of it all. In our role in industrial discussion we should at least be catalysts to contemplation.

4. *Honesty and humility.* We must hold our ideological assumptions before the test of truth and escape from utopian illusions and self-righteous pretensions. A little self-criticism is a valuable thing. Unanswered: What is our test of truth?

Such a list was hardly new, and it might be extended. Some found it useful. I felt strongly, however, that we needed to make judgments about society itself. Otherwise it would be as if Christ spoke to individuals but had nothing to say about the structures that shape their lives. If Christ is Lord of all life—indeed, if God exists at all—He must illumine our thinking about things and organizations as well as individuals.

In pondering the social dimensions of Christianity, the D.I.M. staff made curiously little use of either the concept of the Kingdom of Heaven or the notion of Christian civilization. We merely agreed on our concern to have industrialization evolve so as to produce a more rather than a less human society. And we associated being human with being like Jesus, with a sense of freedom, responsibility for others, and hope. Our basic critique of industrial organizations—both the corporations and the unions—arose from our sense that they distributed power and responsibility so unevenly; that a few men are consumed by these responsibilities and burdened with inordinate power over others, while the majority are given so little responsibility that instead of growing to their full human stature and grasping a modicum of control over their own destinies, they remain stunted. We could affirm American industrialism, not only because of the wealth it produces, but more especially because we believe it can evolve into a system that will distribute power and responsibility more widely. This makes us champions of participative management and union democracy. We further believe that corporations may voluntarily or by govern-

ment pressure enlarge their conception of social responsibility to
include concern for the needs of the whole society, both now and
in future generations.

Our theology, we felt, pointed in these directions. Beyond this
we had many disagreements among ourselves, and even within
these rather general assertions we found much disagreement among
those we knew in industry.

A Stab at Theology

The common experience of facing either uncomprehending
stares or scowls of disagreement among our friends when we tried
to share our theological position with them may have discouraged
us from producing any extensive theological writing. Our theological efforts were at best fragmentary and episodic. Even on the
few occasions when we attempted a comprehensive statement it
emerged brief, sketchy, and—we felt—not generally convincing.
My own best effort resulted from our need to present a secular
statement of the faith to one of our weekend conferences for men
in industry. This came out in the form of five points on purpose,
which I stated as a personal confession. With some hesitation, I
set them down, not because it is a satisfactory summary of my
theological position, but because in a relatively short space it
captures the substance of my orientation at the time.

1. The twentieth century (I said) is nothing if not a time of
rapid change. But this change which is so obvious is not just one
damn thing after another, a tale told by an idiot signifying nothing
—it is a change that has meaning in it. It follows a purposeful
pattern, and this pattern is loaded with possibilities for good. Here
in Detroit, especially, we cannot avoid being intensely aware of
the importance of industry. Perhaps we are so close to it, however,
that we have not fully grasped the fact that the industrial revolution of our time has altered human life and thought more strik-
ingly than any other event since the original development of

agriculture. I believe that this revolution is part of a wonderful Purpose.

An understanding of this Purpose gives me a standard by which to evaluate what is going on in the world at large, and around me in particular. It helps me sort out the more important from the less. It grasps me with a vision and invests me with a sense of urgency. Where I am most aware of this Purpose, I am most conscious of a sense of confidence, freedom, and sometimes even joy. For this Purpose is for good, and therefore, insofar as we are identified with it, nothing can ultimately hurt us.

2. We can be quite clear what this Purpose is. I would define it thus: *All men should grow to their fullest stature in the widest possible fellowship.** The wonderful thing about industrialization is that it has made this Purpose more fully realizable than ever before in history. Of course it will not ever be realized as a final achievement, nor will we ever fully arrive at the ultimate goal. The Purpose is rather that men should experience the *process of growth* toward full humanity. To be growing is—oddly enough—in some sense to be mature. It means acquaintance with painful struggle and new, wonderful, and frightening experiences. It means to be carrying more and more responsibility more adequately. It means to be discovering new dimensions of relationship in old friends and acquaintances. It means to be broadening one's circle of friends into ever new states and areas of society. This will mean more than being an observer of society; it will mean being deeply involved with people personally and being committed to their good. Finally, to grow to its fullest stature, the different sides of personality must unfold. It is not enough to develop toward excellence in one direction. Poetic, artistic, and intuitional expression, as well as economic achievement, are necessary parts of maturity. Fun and play are also parts of life that must not be starved. All these things and more are involved in the human Purpose.

Economic growth seems to be a preoccupation of our country.

* William Temple's definition of God's love.

Our rate of economic growth has been compared unfavorably with that of other industrial countries. All kinds of economic and social policies have been suggested in order to try to stimulate this growth. Public works in the form of schools, hospitals, roads, and higher education for many more young people have been listed as indispensable ingredients for an increased rate of economic growth. In line with my understanding of the purpose of life I should like to propose as a national policy an increased rate of *personal* growth. Broadly recognized, the economy should be developed so as to serve this end.*

3. But the Purpose is not to be achieved through any one means. Everything that happens contributes to it directly or indirectly, positively or negatively. Education, professional life, personal influence—all have a part. Also, however, our political structures, economic organization, and social mores play a part. These make up the environments that enhance or stunt men's growth. True, men influence and shape their environment, but environments shape men as well. All these things are interrelated, so that to change one aspect of life is to influence subtly, profoundly, unexpectedly, all other aspects. Thus the furthering of the Purpose demands action, not only in the sphere of private responsibility and personal encounter but in the realm of political and economic decisions as well.

4. This Purpose of maximum human growth cannot be furthered without a terrific struggle. This struggle is going on now, and it is the key to understanding the conflicts of our time. Industrialization makes it possible to establish the material basis for a life of growth and relationship for all men. The issue at stake is whether this power is going to be used for the benefit of all or for the wealth, power, and privilege of a few. Every issue of con-

---

* This aim is not so strange to us as might appear. Curiously, concern for personal growth not only stands in the best of Christian tradition, but seems to be emerging as an avowed and visible social purpose in such fields as eductation, social work, psychotherapy, and even—along vocational lines—industrial management.

tention in the world around us is related to this question. It is
rarely, of course, simply a question of the bad guys fighting to
preserve their wealth and power against the good guys, who want
all men to share. Often both sides have partially true and adequate,
but conflicting, views about how all men are to be helped to grow.
The struggle is further complicated by the fact that it goes on
continually, not only between groups and individuals, but also
within every individual himself. Something within us resists growth
for ourselves. Growth demands daring and often painful, exhaust-
ing effort. It involves terrifying risks. And therefore we have to be
repeatedly enticed, persuaded, seduced to stick our necks out, to
take chances, to forget our comfort and safety and grow. Perhaps
the hardest thing for us to learn is that in helping others to grow,
we ourselves grow most profoundly.

5. It is possible to relate ourselves to the Purpose. We are given
the opportunity in life to cooperate with it. We can become an
active force in creating organizations in which people can grow
and in encouraging others to grow themselves. And in so doing
we find the meaning in life. This cooperation demands first of all
personal *reflection*. This is a habit which we tend not to cultivate.
It involves looking at our life and the world around us and dis-
cerning how the Purpose is working itself out, where new possibilities are about to be realized, and how I in my own life can
further its realization. This requires us all to develop a capacity
not only for honest and realistic introspection, but also for social
analysis and *social criticism*.

Second, cooperation with the Purpose involves *communication*
with others about its meaning. We need to share the fruits of our
individual reflection. This is particularly significant when it takes
place across class, occupational, racial, or national lines. Such
sharing may greatly enrich our own understanding, but over and
above this, the process of sharing is itself a part of the realization
of the Purpose.

Third, reflection and communication imply *action*. This is the conscious cooperation of the individual with Purpose. It may take place in a great variety of areas of public and private life. It may involve making decisions significantly changing the lives of thousands. It may involve relating in a profoundly human fashion to one other person. Most of us, most of the time, do not have the power to change very much in our environment. But more often than we realize, we all do have the opportunity to push the life of our society a little bit, perhaps only a tiny little bit, in the direction of growth toward more abundant, dignified, beautiful human living. Even this is significant.

And in this (I said) we can rejoice.

But having said this, I was nevertheless well aware that if I were to move to Boston I would be leaving the task of theological interpretation hardly begun. It did not make the decision any easier.

CRISIS AND HOPE

At first I thought I wanted to refuse the new opportunity. I had been seven years in Detroit, had made many friends and grown to like it, and in spite of periodic difficulties with the rest of the D.I.M. staff, we had somehow worked out a modus operandi which promised well for the progress of the mission.

But finally I decided to go.

I was intrigued as well as a little frightened by the challenge. I felt that since D.I.M. was on the tracks, established, institutionalized, and world famous, my experience and such skill as I had might now be more urgently needed in Boston. While Sheffield industry was old-fashioned and Detroit's contemporary, the electronics industry around Boston might bode significantly for the future. At least it was a new kind of industry, with new problems and opportunity for new ideas. It required, I thought, a new kind of industrial mission. I found the challenge exciting.

Harvey Cox, Mike Bloy, and the rest of the board in Boston seemed to have a conception of the job which was extremely congenial to me. The situation drew me, for it seemed possible that even of myself it might require growth in directions I had perhaps not dreamed of before. And I had to admit that the thought of returning to New England was appealing. Moreover, although I hope it was not a major ingredient in my decision, I felt some desire to create a piece of work on my own. (Ambition can be an ugly thing if it is allowed to override other considerations.)

Although I left Detroit confident in the future of D.I.M., I had also a sense of ongoing crisis. We had not made much progress in developing a theology appropriate for industrial society, yet I felt painfully that this problem was critical. Three experiences gave sharpened weight to my feeling.

Item 1. One Sunday not many months before I left for Boston I found the litany sung in procession at St. Joseph's intensely moving. A flood of associations filled me with a sense of historical continuity between our situation today and the many Christians of past ages. I thought of Augustine and his monks singing litanies as they went across the Kentish fields on their way to Canterbury. I thought of the deathbed scenes in Bede's *Ecclesiastical History.* I thought of the "battles, murders, and sudden deaths, the plagues, pestilence and famines" of medieval Europe. I thought of the terrible struggles of the monks with themselves, and the bitter conflicts of the Reformation. Somehow, before the litany was over, my eyes were wet with tears. I *felt* the truth and beauty of the Gospel and of the Christian experience with a kind of deep, indescribable directness. No argument was needed to persuade me of it.

And yet, looking around, I knew that the associations that made the service so moving to me were probably not in the minds of most of those present. In fact, those who reach back into history in their feeling are probably somewhat unusual in the modern world. And since most people are simply not moved by these things, the communication of Christian faith cannot depend on this kind of historical sensitivity.

Item 2. I was flattered when Arthur Kornhauser, a professor of industrial sociology, not only borrowed my journals but phoned to say that he had read them with great interest and wanted to talk with me about them.

One of his first remarks when we met was, "Well, I see you've got some problems. Although I was most interested in your industrial experiences and observations, I still don't really understand what you hope to do religiously. I can't possibly see that Christianity can make any contribution to the life of industry."

I tried to explain once again that the social teaching of the Church offers criteria by which to judge society and points the direction toward which it should move; that the faith offers the possibility of a spiritual dynamic which can move men to live courageously, significantly, and sacrificially.

"But, of course," he answered, "men can equally find such things outside religion. There are wonderful men with a profound understanding of society who are not in the least religious or theologically minded. And in fact the Church with its silly supernatural baggage and its tendency toward narrow bigotry and otherworldliness has often done more harm than good. Religion makes less and less sense to modern men, and though I agree with you that we need a 'moral equivalent of religion' we must find it in the realm of rational thinking."

I realized that I was not communicating with him at all on the theological level and said to him, "You, and men like you, are the epitome of our problem. If we can learn to talk about the faith so that it makes sense to you, we will have gone a long way toward achieving our goal."

Although I was sure he knew that his scientific research had produced little positive result, and that he himself had dismally failed to communicate significantly to the mass of "practical" industrialists, the difference was that he saw himself on the winning side and me on the losing one. In fact, he said he would not be surprised in time to see me leave the ministry and go into teaching.

It occurred to me that *industrial mission is a kind of last-ditch effort to relate the faith significantly to modern society.*

I might easily judge Kornhauser's optimism about the future of rational intelligence to be naïve. Much evidence suggests that this is so. Nevertheless, the only reason I could give him for holding to our "silly supernaturalisms" was that I believed them to be true. And no reason I gave as to why they were true would convince him.

"He who has ears, let him hear."

But what about the increasing multitude without ears?

Item 3. A close friend left his post as a chaplain at a university, left the ministry, and returned to a job in industry. To explain the reasons for his resignation, he wrote an extremely frank paper in which he described his personal anxieties at being in a situation without a supporting institutional structure, a viable style of life, or a recognized identity. And most of all, he confessed that on the secular campus he found it not merely difficult to believe in the Christian gospel, but practically impossible *to perceive what the gospel really was.* He also attacked his seminary for seeming to lead him on to think that the meaning of the gospel was clear, that he could appropriate it for himself and relate it to life if he would only be a little more pious, a little more learned, or a little more humble.

I am convinced that the Christian faith is facing a climate of opinion in industrial America which is far more inimical to it than the Church generally realizes. We cannot face the truth. Our seminaries are really brainwashing institutions. For a man to appropriate the faith inwardly to a degree where he can build his life upon it, he has to isolate himself in a community with a special discipline, atmosphere, and style of life so as to make the verities of the faith to seem credible. And then he generally buries himself in the institutional Church, where he finds the maximum psychological support for his beliefs. From this sheltered vantage point he proclaims that Christ is Lord of all life and that Christianity speaks to all men in every area of their living. I wonder if his faith could flourish if he lived as a layman in the hurly-burly of a competitive secular institution. Most of the laymen I know in this kind of situation preserve their faith by not expecting much from it. *They do not demand that it relate significantly to their competitive weekday life and to the society at large.* And so they are not disappointed.

The situation reminds me of a report I once read on the ecology of Scotland. Apparently at one time the climate on the coast was warmer and dryer. Great conifer forests grew and covered the hills. They survived long after the climate changed, because the forest itself gave the individual trees shelter from the vicissitudes of the weather. But then the forests were cut down, and new young trees, finding the weather too harsh, have not been able to grow. The only exception is where the Forestry Commission has given artificial help by building fences against the wind.

The historian Carl Becker seems to have been thinking along the same lines when he wrote, in 1932, "Theology, or something that goes by that name, is still kept alive by the faithful, but only by artificial respiration." I wondered if this was in fact our condition.

After reading my journal a friend, Henry Hager, said he was fascinated by D.I.M.'s work but a little saddened by it. "The tragedy is that you are doomed to failure. I cannot conceive of your really influencing the life or direction of industry even by a hair's breadth," was his comment. (So might an ancient have spoken, looking at the first handful of early Christians confronting the Roman Empire.)

I had to admit that he might possibly be right, yet I did not share his sadness. Much of what I experienced in Detroit industry seemed to confirm Becker's hypothesis. That we had not yet become a force in shaping modern industrial society goes almost comically without saying. These chapters have described what might be looked on as a pilot experiment. It was carried out over a very few years and in very few locations. Yet the level of success attained—however scattered and patchy it may appear—was, I believe, no mean achievement and one on which further achievements must build.

What these may be will depend not only on the effectiveness of missions such as D.I.M. and others elsewhere, some already in existence, but on the kind of support they are given by the church. To me at least it seems clear that if the church had developed this kind of mission on a wide front a decade earlier, the history of the labor movement itself might have been different. Certainly these beginnings and partial successes will become significant only to the extent that the church builds on them in the future on a larger scale.

On the personal side, the romantic in me used sometimes to think darkly of an heroic struggle against impossible odds—of becoming a failure for Christ's sake. But this is mere momentary coloring. We do not know the future. To grapple with the most important human issues is profoundly exhilarating, and to have one's small successes in terms of vital human experience, leading to further insight, is a wonderful thing. If there is great danger of failure here, I must still say that what may look like sacrifice to others, to me is nothing of the kind.

While still in Sheffield I told a German visitor as we left a plant discussion, "Pastor Poelcher, you see, in this post-Christian culture we cannot preach the gospel directly as Billy Graham does, but only indirectly by sharing concern for social problems."

"On the contrary," he replied, "it is you who are preaching the gospel directly and Billy Graham who does it indirectly."

Certainly Poelcher's comment is as debatable as it is intriguing. Nevertheless, there is a certain kind of immediacy involved in an effort to live out and preach the gospel, not so much through the old familar words as through life itself, in a very concrete modern setting unconnected with religious thought. This is especially true in the world of industry, whose complex structure seems often to collide with Christian feeling and insights and to create conflict accordingly.

For here both a kind of preaching and effective living must be done in the end (and soon), or nothing will come of it all. "What the world expects of Christians," says Albert Camus, "is that Christians should speak out loud and clear. . . . The grouping we need is a grouping of men resolved to speak out clearly and pay up personally. . . ."* But he suggests that perhaps, instead, Christianity will insist on compromise, on obscuring its insights in deference to the world.

"In that case, Christians will live and Christianity will die."

Our groping efforts to touch and release men's minds, and to communicate in their own terms, may not seem like speaking out loud and clear. But without such efforts how can we begin? We met men in their real experience. We began there.

And the force of it, the loudness so that all can hear, is not unconnected ultimately with courage and patience and persistence. Thus I believe the truth of Becker's statement and of my friend's, above, will depend on whether or not there are those who will carry on such work, in sufficient volume and in the necessary stages of its unfolding, whatever the cost.

* *Resistance, Rebellion, and Death* (New York: Alfred A. Knopf, 1960), p. 71.